ANCIENT IRELAND

ANCIENT IRELAND

NICK CONSTABLE

CHARTWELL
BOOKS, INC.

ACKNOWLEDGMENTS

The photographs for this book were kindly supplied by Bord Failte, the Irish Tourist Board except for the following: the National Museum of Ireland provided those on pp35, 36/37 (Top), 54 (Below left and right), 66 and 67; John Cleare those on pp18/19, 45, 46, 47, 50, 51, 56 and 57.

Photograph Page 1: *The Rock of Cashel, Co Tipperary.*
Photograph Page 2: *The coast at Youghal, Co Cork.*

This edition first published in 1996 by the
Promotional Reprint Company Ltd,
Kiln House,
210 New Kings Road,
London SW6 4NZ.

Copyright
Text © Promotional Reprint Company Ltd 1996
Layout and Design © Promotional Reprint Company Ltd 1996

CHARTWELL BOOKS. INC.
A division of BOOK SALES, INC
P.O. Box 7100
Edison, New Jersey 08818-7100

ISBN 0 7858 0689 X

Printed and bound in China

CONTENTS

INTRODUCTION

Ireland has always been a land of troubles. From the constant squabbling of the early Gaelic chieftains, through to the barbarism of the Vikings, the ruthless military efficiency of the Normans, and the twisted logic of Oliver Cromwell's religious bigotry, the island has known hardly a decade's peace in 2,000 years. Today, in spite of courageous attempts by democratic politicians to find a lasting solution to the nationalist/unionist divide, the shadow of conflict hangs as dark as ever over the country.

But this is not a book about Ireland's present sad plight, however closely the problems of partition can be linked to the actions of previous centuries. Instead, it aims to find defining moments in Irish history up to the 18th century and look at how these have shaped the country's distinctive culture and environment. Inevitably, the legacies of past wars feature heavily. To many of the old Celtic kings, war was their whole reason for being; an affirmation of their power and a constant source of inspiration to their historians, poets and storytellers.

It must also be said that Ireland is a place worth fighting for: anyone who has seen an Atlantic storm hit the rugged west coast, strolled along the hauntingly beautiful yellow beaches, watched sunlight spearing the clouds onto purple-clad mountains, smelled the peat fires of the villages and the sweet, rain-washed air, tramped the wild boglands and watched the mist roll in across peaceful loughs; anyone who has experienced one or more of these things knows something of the magic of the place.

It is worth looking briefly at the geography of Ireland, if only to do some scene-setting for the historical events considered later in the book. In very general terms, the country looks like a saucer with jagged edges — its central limestone plains surrounded on almost every side by dramatic mountain scenery. Aside from the lowland midlands, with its bogs and gentle pastureland, a journey through the Irish countryside produces a constantly changing panorama. Travelling across the Silvermine mountains, near Nenagh, for instance, you can find yourself moving from craggy heights into Tipperary's rolling dairy country within the space of a few miles. Similarly, a car ride across the Mayo plains, beneath the rounded mass of Ben Nephin, will take you quickly into one of the country's most desolate districts — the peatlands of the north-west.

Irish mountains, particularly, are inspiring. Because the ranges are small and set in isolated groups around the plains, they seem to tower much higher than their 610-915m (2-3,000ft) would suggest. Each range has its own character, the result of very different geological processes, and so the sandstone ridge and valley scenery of the south-east is a striking contrast to the volcanic basalt of Antrim or the glistening quartzite of mountains such as Mayo's Croagh Patrick or Donegal's Errigal.

The Ice Age also left its mark on the landscape, particularly in the lowlands. Here features such as eskers and drumlins — geological terms derived from Gaelic words — can be easily spotted. Eskers are low, curving ridges of gravelly soil deposited by rivers of melting ice over thousands of years. They were among the first early trackways, providing a firm footing across marshy wetlands, and some Irish roads still follow them. One of the most interesting eskers, called the Pilgrim's Road, runs for several miles along the Shannon's east bank from the old monastery at Clonmacnoise to the Shannonbridge crossing.

Drumlins are long, low, narrow mounds of rock and soil built up by the glaciers and aligned along the direction of the ice flow. Some of the best examples are found in Co Down but they can be seen throughout the western and northern limits of the central lowlands.

Although the land itself has changed little since the days of Ireland's first inhabitants, the scenery is drastically different. This is largely because the native deciduous woodland which covered most of the country was ruthlessly hacked down during the early days of British colonialism. The British navy earmarked the best oaks for its frigates (ancient woodland around Lough Derg, on the River Shannon, proved particularly popular for this) and vast tracts of forest were cut for iron-smelting charcoal. When, in later years, English landlords began fencing off their estates and reclaiming forests for agriculture, the Irish peasants had little choice but to strip unenclosed woods for their building materials and their fuel. The effect has been to turn today's Ireland into one of the least wooded of all European countries. Where forests once flourished, the land now bears a man-made creation of patchwork fields divided by neat stone walls and hedgerows.

The country's main industry is, and always has been, farming. Agricultural land is best in the east and south-east where good quality soils allow some large arable farms. The further west you go, the more the soil deteriorates. Here the focus is on livestock farming — dairy and beef cattle on the pasture and sheep on the open moors and mountains. It is this concentration on farming which has helped keep the Irish countryside economically buoyant and, as a result, the population is evenly spread. Even in the wildernesses of the north and west, farms and cottages can usually be seen and small towns and villages are scattered almost everywhere. Indeed, apart from Dublin and Belfast, Ireland has no major cities and only towns such as Cork, Limerick, Waterford and Derry can be considered large by European standards.

Opposite: *The Caha Mountains in Co Cork. The range is among the most evocative sights in all Ireland, rising from the shores of Bantry Bay to reach heights of 610m (2,000ft) and above.*

Ireland has four main provinces — Munster in the south, Connacht in the west, Leinster in the east and Ulster in the north — comprising 32 counties. It would take too long to do justice to each region's character (and in any case this is not a travel guide) but a brief summary should help readers unfamiliar with Ireland to put the various historical sites mentioned later into context.

We begin in the north with the whole of Ulster — that is the six United Kingdom counties of Antrim, Armagh, Down, Fermanagh, Londonderry and Tyrone as well as the Irish Republic counties of Donegal, Monaghan and Cavan This region is dominated by Belfast, although outside the city it is a rural area of high rolling hills, rugged coastal stretches and, in the west, glorious beaches. In Donegal the mountain peaks running on a north-east to south-west axis are among the most inhospitable in the country and settlements are consequently few and far between. Lough Neagh, which borders Antrim, Armagh and Tyrone, is the largest lake in the British Isles covering a surface area of some 380sq km (147sq.miles.).

South and west of Ulster lies the Atlantic coastal district of Connemara, part of Co Galway and Co Mayo in Connacht. This is a country of forbidding granite moorlands and quartzite mountains, broken by innumerable lakes and river valleys. Beyond Lough Mask lie the heights of the Nephin Beg range, with its tallest peak, Ben Nephin, rising majestically above Lough Conn and Lough Cullin. North-east of Mayo, beyond the Ox Mountains, is Co Sligo with its mixture of pasture and bogland, and Co Roscommon, where the southward-flowing River Shannon proved such a significant frontier during ancient conflicts.

Further down the west coast there is The Burren, a limestone plateau in which rough, stony fields occasionally give way to outcrops of white rocks. The plateau ends at the Cliffs of Moher, high above the Atlantic, from where to the north-west the three storm-lashed islands of Aran can be seen huddling together.

Southwards, beyond the Shannon estuary, lies Munster and the mountains of Cork and Kerry — perhaps Ireland's best-loved scenery. Here the spectacular Slieve Mish and Derrynasaggart ranges sandwich the lavishly-named Macgillycuddy's Reeks where the country's highest peak, the 1,041m (3,415ft) Carrantuohil, towers above the lakes of Killarney. This landscape has always proved hostile to invading armies. It may be wild country, but in past years it was one of the most important refuges for Gaelic resistance.

Moving east the traveller comes to the South Country and the counties of Tipperary, Waterford and Kilkenny. Here mountains such as the Knockmealdowns, the Comeraghs, the Monavullaghs and the Galteers again dominate the countryside, although views are softened by the beautiful pastoral valleys of the Suir and Blackwater rivers. To the north the Silvermines mountains sweep down to the largest of the Shannon lakes, Lough Derg.

Leinster's eastern seaboard is as dramatic as anywhere in Ireland. The Wicklow Hills rise directly out of the sea a few miles south of Dublin and form a massif well over 350m (1,148ft) high. This exposed, open moorland has few river valleys and must have been a formidable barrier to troop movements down the ages. Only the narrow coastal strip between Dublin and Co Wexford provides a reasonably flat north-south route.

West and north of Dublin is the great central plain known as the Midlands, which rarely rises above 100m (328ft). It was once a gigantic bog (terrain hated by the English armies) but has gradually been reclaimed as fertile agricultural land.

Above: *The ancient art of turf cutting is still common in much of rural Ireland. Here a family from Achill, Co Mayo, load up for the trip home.*

So much for the shape of the land. Geography and geology are mostly exact sciences and there is little room for argument and speculation over interpretation. History, (especially Irish history) however, is a different matter again. Here the problem is too much biased interpretation, coupled with a tendency among the early 'praise poets' to habitually over-egg the pudding. Contemporary accounts of just about any early historical event in Ireland have to be read with an eye to the writer's own interests — specifically the patronage offered him by his lord and master.

This book begins with the very first Stone Age inhabitants, the men and women who are the only citizens of 'pure' Irish stock that the land has ever known. There are some romantic tales which more than suggest that Ireland was 'taken' by a wave of intrepid Celt invaders, a people who became the nation's founding fathers. In fact all the historical evidence suggests this scenario is distinctly questionable. The Celts, as we shall see, were just another bunch of warriors with colonial ambitions. They do not appear to have seized the land by force, but then they didn't need to. At the time the Celts began arriving from Britain and France the native population of Ireland must have been so small as to be almost insignificant. Even if they'd wanted a fight they would have had to look hard to find an enemy. Most likely Celtic colonisation was a gradual process which happened peacefully over hundreds if not thousands of years.

The sad truth is that our knowledge of early Irish history remains terribly sketchy. Up until recently, most archaeologists were still insisting that the Romans never invaded the country. They explained away Roman hoards and artifacts and a Romano-

British grave as the result of sporadic trading and exploration. Then in 1996 came confirmation of a massive fortified settlement at Drumanagh, which seems to have been a beach-head for the Roman army on campaign in Ireland. At a stroke, a whole swathe of domestic historical theory was exposed as fundamentally flawed. While this is no fault of the archaeologists, who can work only with the information available, it is a useful reminder that few things about this period are certain.

Above: *Once the haunt of outlaws and tribal bands, the Ring of Kerry is now tramped by thousands of visitors every year. This view shows a stretch of the rocky coast near Cahirdaniel.*

British grave as the result of sporadic trading and exploration. Then in 1996 came confirmation of a massive fortified settlement at Drumanagh, which seems to have been a beach-head for the Roman army on campaign in Ireland. At a stroke, a whole swathe of domestic historical theory was exposed as fundamentally flawed. While this is no fault of the archaeologists, who can work only with the information available, it is a useful reminder that few things about this period are certain.

The decline of the late Roman Empire may have given Irish Celts the confidence to conquer new lands of their own. They took control of Scotland through the Dál Riata, a tribe from Co Antrim, and there is good evidence that Irish tribes from Munster, such as the Dési and the Úi Liatháin, settled in western Britain from north Wales down as far as Devon and Cornwall. Perhaps this Celtish invasion was to assist the Britons in driving the Romans out — although around this time Irish warriors were also attacking the west of Britain simply to plunder and loot any settlements they could find. It was on one such raid that they captured a young boy from a wealthy family and took him home to work as a slave. In later years, Irish nationalists imbued with a romantic view of their heritage, must have shuddered at this cruel twist of history. To think that the most famous of all Irish saints, St Patrick, was a Brit!

Once the Romans had been forced out of Ireland, the country was temporarily free of any further outside hostility. But there was certainly no peace. Gaelic tribes lived in a state of constant war with each other and the internal politics of the following 500 years is a maelstrom of confusion. There would be occasions when some leader with enough military clout would declare himself 'High King' of Ireland, a title which usually meant little outside his immediate sphere of influence. However the Úi Néills dynasty, the country's most powerful tribe, were able to make their claim for kingship stick over very large areas indeed, especially during the 9th century. As we shall see Ireland came very close to uniting under a single king, although it never actually happened.

The Viking wars, which began at the end of the 8th century, had a devastating effect on the Christian communities of Ireland. Monastery after monastery was sacked, whole villages were razed and the country's greatest treasures exported back to Scandinavia. At first Gaelic coastal settlements were helpless against such fast, sea-borne raids but later the tribes began to hit back with some success.

Fears that the country would be over-run by Vikings during the middle of the 9th century proved groundless and although the long-boats returned early in the 10th century this second period of raiding lasted little more than two decades. One of the greatest battles in Irish history took place at this time — the Battle of Dublin (919). This engagement has sometimes been portrayed as a showdown between the greatest of the Úi Néill warriors and the cream of the Dublin-based Vikings. In fact, petty rivalries and jealousies meant the makeup of the two sides was actually far more complicated, with Viking fighting Viking and Irishman fighting Irishman.

For all their undoubted military and economic strength, the Vikings imprinted surprisingly little of their culture on the Irish way. True, their language is credited with naming three of the four provinces (Munster, Ulster and Leinster) and some towns such as Dublin, Waterford, Wexford, Wicklow, Howth and Carlingford were named from Old Norse words. But aside from this, and a few words borrowed for the Gaelic language, there is surprisingly little to remember them by. Perhaps their greatest positive achievement was the maritime trade they brought to Ireland. Dublin at this time was one of the most important ports of the Viking world and was the centre of many trade routes. This might seem odd to us today because the city is seen as something of a European outpost. But in Viking times Dublin held a key position as a halfway stop-over between Gibralter and Norway. Despite the huge distances involved, navigators of the day seem to have been well used to the sea lanes.

The next group of colonial hopefuls to land were the Normans. At first sight it might be thought their seizure of Ireland was the result of some carefully worked-out political strategy. Nothing could be further from the truth. It was a random, haphazard, chaotic affair in which successive English kings turned out to have very little say. Even when Henry II landed near Waterford in October 1171 at the head of a large army it was as much to keep his own barons under control as seize new territory for the Crown. Over the preceding two years the ousted Irish king of Leinster, Dermot MacMurrough, had recruited some mercenary Norman lords to help him reclaim his kingdom (including Dublin). Such was their degree of success that Henry saw the dangers of a powerful new kingdom arising on his vulnerable western borders. His very presence was enough to bring both Irish and Norman leaders into line beneath his rule.

Yet the problem for the English king and his successors, was keeping them there. As more and more Norman barons began flooding in to Ireland to claim estates, it became apparent that they cared little for any edicts issued by some far-distant monarch. This was a time of rising population in Europe — and therefore rising food prices — and the barons wasted no time cashing in. They guarded their investments by building motte and bailey castles (for which they received feudal grants from the Crown) and, almost by accident, completed a highly effective colonisation of the country. This was fine in times of plenty — but when populations began to fall, and Europe became devastated by plague, many of the barons abandoned their Irish estates and headed home to more comfortable country seats in England. From the middle of the 14th century there arose a revival in Gaelic culture — and outbreaks of civil war among Irish chieftains jockeying for positions of power.

Throughout this book the theme of religious freedom and the survival instincts of the Catholic Church, crop up time and again. The Viking raids were a dark time for the priests, but these were as nothing in comparison to the systematic persecution which lay ahead. When Henry VIII set the Reformation in train he tried to impose his model of the English Church onto Ireland and set about replacing his Catholic government officials — even though their loyalty to the Crown was absolute. For many of these Catholics this was a time of traumatic personal conflict. Their king demanded they should recognise his spiritual authority; their church demanded that they should not. Attempts by some Dublin lawyers to find a compromise were doomed from the start and the seeds of 400 years of religious strife were duly sown in fertile soil.

The mutual mistrust between England and Ireland deepened under Elizabeth I with the establishment of the first Protestant settlements or 'plantations'. For decades there was no let-up in the siege mentality prevailing among Irish Catholics, who were soon confronted with a deluge of aggressive new Protestant colonisers taking advantage of iniquitous laws to grab land and property when and wherever they could. In the first few decades of the 17th century at least 100,000 Britons crossed the Irish Sea to make new lives for themselves. By 1641 the Catholic lords could take no more, and they retaliated by becoming the persecutors. At least 2,000 Protestants were slaughtered and thousands more were stripped of their clothes and turned out into the streets. Such appalling acts were further exaggerated by church leaders in England and Scotland to the point where it was believed the Irish had massacred virtually every Protestant in Ireland.

It was against this background of suspicion and hatred that the most formidable army in Europe, headed by Oliver Cromwell, arrived in Ireland intent on revenge. It was an army fuelled and fired by a combination of religious zeal and an eagerness for plundering and it reminded Catholics everywhere of their perilous position under a Protestant monarch. Not until the crowning of James II, a Catholic king, in 1685 would there be a general sense of relief.

It is with the removal of James II from the English throne in 1688, and his failed attempt to regain it from Ireland, that this book ends. James' defeat by William of Orange in the two key battles of the 'Glorious Revolution' — at the Boyne in 1690 and Aughrim the following year — ushered in the era of Ascendancy, a culture in which wealth, land, education and the best jobs became Protestant luxuries and in which the poor would be thrown to the mercy of poverty, disease and famine.

The chapters ahead are not intended to give an exhaustive account of Irish history before the 18th century. Neither do they try to draw lofty conclusions about the reasons for today's republican-versus-unionist conflict. The aim is rather to offer a glimpse of Ireland's colourful and fascinating past, of some of her sufferings and her triumphs but, most of all, of the people who made her.

Opposite above: *The still of the evening captured at Lough Talt, Co Sligo.*

Opposite below: *A reminder of Ireland's war torn past at Rosslare, Co Wexford. The south-east coast saw many invasions — from the first Celts to the 'shock troops' of Oliver Cromwell.*

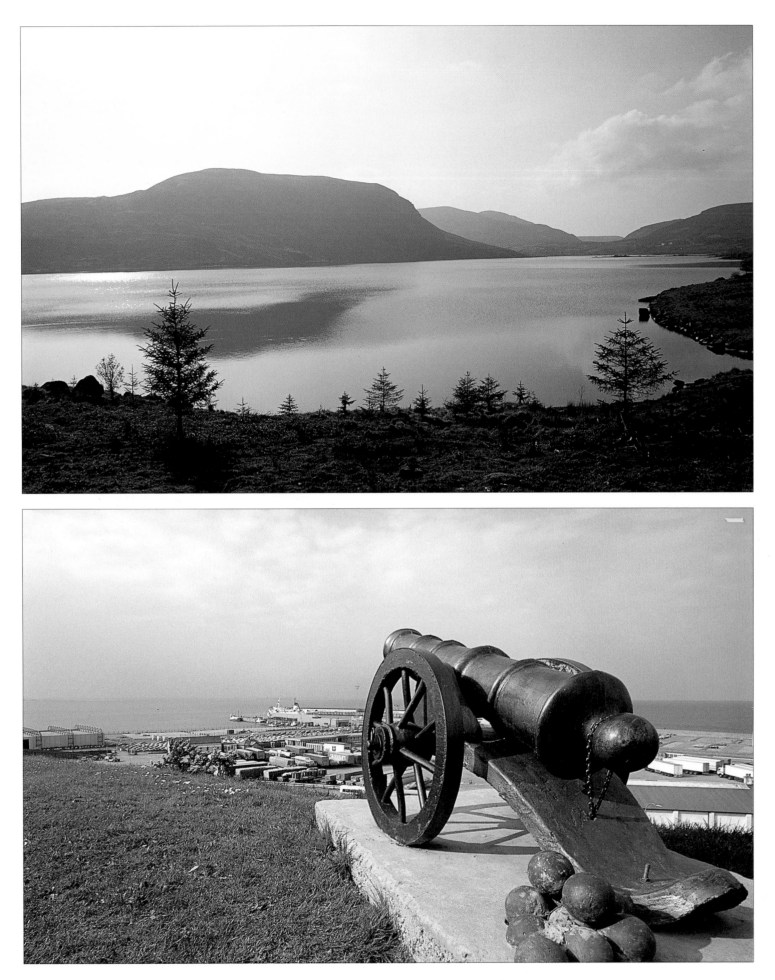

THE FIRST PEOPLE

Throughout the Ice Age, which lasted from about 1.7 million years ago to around 11,000BC Ireland was geographically linked to the European continent. For much of this time the country was covered by an ice cap, which advanced and retreated according to the various warm and cold phases in global weather patterns. It is possible that a population established itself during one or other of the warm spells, although there is no evidence for this yet. Present thinking is that the first humans in Ireland arrived somewhere between 8000BC and 6500BC and that they crossed from Britain along one of several land bridges that existed at the time. Many wild animals also made the crossing but some, such as beavers, roe deer, wild cattle, otters and snakes never made it over in time (to this day there are no snakes in Ireland). As the climate warmed, so the ice melted and sea levels rose — causing the land bridges to disappear forever beneath the waves.

These first human settlers were hunter-gatherers. From analysis of settlements such as Mount Sandel, in Co Derry, they seem to have dined on the likes of duck, pigeon and grouse, along with nuts and berries. Fish was also a major part of their diet — the remains of eels, flounder, salmon and sea bass have all been identified at Mount Sandel — and pig and hare may have been hunted with the help of dogs. Weapons were mainly flint arrows and spears, although stone axes were also made — most notably from factories at Tievebulliagh and on the isle of Rathlin in Co Antrim. These porcellanite axes were probably Ireland's first large-scale exports and have turned up in far-flung archaeological sites right across the British Isles.

The early Stone Age Irish would have spent much of their time on the move, seeking out new hunting grounds in winter and then perhaps returning to established sources of food in summer. Ulster and Leinster probably saw the first colonies, but exploration inland must have been severely limited by the dense forests and scrub. Lakes and rivers were the only way to travel at speed.

Initial colonisation of Ireland was followed by the second key event in the country's pre-history — the development of agriculture and a more stable, ordered existence. Farming techniques were adopted in Ireland somewhere around the 4th millennium BC, spreading from the Middle East where they had emerged some 3,000 years earlier. The first Irish farmers began enthusiastically clearing forest for cultivation and by 3400BC the first farm animals had been introduced. Cattle, sheep and goats seem to have been brought over in an already domesticated state by settlers arriving from Britain. The prevailing theory is that these Neolithic colonists came from south-west Scotland to the counties of Antrim and Down, which they could see on a good day with the naked eye over the North Channel. Longer voyages may have been made further south across the Irish Sea, but the chances of cattle surviving in small open boats, their legs tethered, must have been much slimmer.

Above: *Staigue Fort, Co Kerry, is one of a number of early stone fortresses which may have been influenced by Scottish designs.*

Opposite: *The so-called 'Bog Roads', such as this one in Co Longford, were a communications lifeline for the early Irish. Much of the land was either impenetrable forest or impassable marsh.*

One of the oldest known Neolithic houses in either Britain or Ireland has been excavated at Ballynagilly, near Cookstown, Co Tyrone. It dates from about 3200BC and was square-shaped, covering around 40sq m (430ft). The walls were formed of planks of oak driven into a shallow trench and the roof was probably thatch. Later houses used stone foundations with wattle-and-daub packed between wooden posts.

While these domestic houses are now little more than chemical remains in the soil, there are plenty of surviving monuments on which we can judge the skills of the megalithic builders. Their great tombs, stone circles and standing stones are among the most evocative features of the Irish landscape. The sheer scale of these early engineering projects still inspires wonder today.

The geological wonderland that is Craig Cave at Castleisland, Co. Kerry.

TOMBS, CIRCLES AND STONES

Beneath its fertile soil Ireland has one of the richest archaeological treasure troves anywhere in Europe. This is partly because less intensive farming methods over the years have helped preserve the past. But it is also down to the sheer productivity of the ancient megalithic builders. There are at least 1,200 known megalithic monuments in Ireland and probably many more which have disappeared over the years.

This area of pre-history is sometimes forgotten by those who seek to establish the 'real identity' of the Irish. It is probable that the first megalithic builders arrived from France in two or three distinct waves, absorbing into the resident population slowly and smoothly. They were a people whose customs and beliefs, rituals and laws are unclear to us today. But bearing in mind the scale of the building projects they undertook (*megalith* means 'large stone' in Greek), they must have been not only committed and resourceful but also driven by some powerful faith.

Most megalithic monuments in Ireland were built somewhere between 2000 and 3000BC, although modern radio-carbon dating methods are not always accurate. There appear to be four main types:

• Court Cairns: Well over 300 of these have now been identified, mostly north of a line between Galway and Dundalk. Only about a tenth of them have been properly excavated but the items recovered are much the same. They include cremated human bones, typical round-bottomed 'Western Neolithic' pots, flint and chert arrowheads and the odd axe or knife.

The purpose of court cairns is debatable. Very little pottery is ever found intact, suggesting either that many tombs were disturbed by later peoples or that their contents were moved in from earlier burial sites (perhaps to appease the spirits and nature gods). The cairns consist of a narrow mound of earth with a small courtyard at one end leading into a narrow passageway. The passage is often sectioned off into a series of chambers.

It is likely that these tombs were the pagan equivalent of a parish church, acting as a cult centre for communities of around 50-100 people all living within a couple of miles radius. Perhaps the cairns were a way of establishing ancestral rights over a particular ground. Certainly, studies of megaliths in Co Leitrim suggest that they were positioned on light, well-drained, upland soils ideally suited to early farming practice. This implies that they stood close to domestic settlements as important focal points for the communities they served. Among the most interesting are at Creevykeel and Treanmacmurtagh in Co Sligo, Ballyalton and Audleystown in Co Down, and Browndod in Co Antrim.

• Portal Tombs (also known as dolmens): These are the most dramatic of the Irish megaliths and something no visitor to the country should miss. They are above-ground tombs and one theo-

Above: *Proleek Dolmen, a typical portal tomb at Ballymascanlon, and (**Opposite**) another fine example at Haroldstown, Co Carlow. The word Dolmen comes from an old Breton phrase meaning 'stone table'.*

ry is that they evolved out of the court cairn design (the sites of the two types closely tally). When seen against the skyline, portal tombs can eerily evoke the magic of Ireland's mysterious past and it is little wonder they became an integral part of the nation's folklore. Who could blame later peoples for believing them to be the dining tables of giants? — The term dolmen originates from old Breton words meaning stone and table — and no doubt their massive capstones were designed to impress Neolithic tribesmen. Some of these stones weighed 102kg (100 tons) or more and appear to have been hauled into place on wooden rollers. The number of willing hands needed to pull them the final few metres up a temporary earthen ramp is a matter of guesswork, but it was possibly several hundred.

Portal tombs were often built close to the sea and along river valleys. Good examples include Legananny, Co Down, Kilclooney, Co Donegal and Ballykeel, Co Armagh.

• Passage Tombs: These were perhaps the first great architectural designs of prehistoric European culture. They rank alongside the temples of Malta in importance and are Western Europe's modest equivalent of the Egyptian pyramids or the Mycenaean burial chambers (the idea of an above-ground passage and tomb covered with an artificial mound is the same). Passage tombs are usually found in countries bordering the eastern Atlantic, such as Portugal, Spain, France, Scandinavia, Wales, Scotland and, of course, Ireland.

The Irish examples are arguably the most fascinating. They tend to be sited together in large cemeteries such as Newgrange, Knowth and Dowth and Loughcrew in Co Meath, and Carrowmore and Carrowkeel in Co Sligo. Often there is one very large tomb easily distinguishable from the others — almost as a cathedral among a scattering of churches. These larger versions are not always found in the centre of a cemetery. At Knocknarea near Sligo town the grave of Queen Maeve looks down on smaller passage tombs making up the main Carrowmore cluster.

Studies of the tombs have shown that they were used both for cremation and burial rituals. The Irish Tourist Board archaeologist Patrick Hartnett established that the one at Fourknocks, Co Meath, contained the remains of some 60 people, yet these bodies would not have been interred in one mass service. Rather, passage tombs were the equivalent of the graveyard vaults used by wealthy families of recent times. Passage tombs were mostly a final resting place for several different generations, although some may have been constructed specifically for a great tribal chief.

The items placed with the dead are more difficult to fathom. In addition to the usual pottery, there are often carved bone pins which may have fastened leather bags containing the cremated remains of the dead. As these pins are usually burnt, however, it's perhaps more likely that they clasped a cloak around a dead body as

it lay on a funeral pyre. Other grave goods include stone pendants or talismans, usually made out of soapstone or limestone and often fashioned in the shape of a hammer or axe. Most enigmatic of all are the large balls of chalk or stone which have turned up. Their significance remains a mystery.

Sadly, some of the secrets of the passage tombs may already have been lost for ever. So called 'excavations' (which in reality were little more than grave robberies) of the 19th and early 20th centuries destroyed much vital archaeological material. One of the worst cases occurred at the remarkable Loughcrew passage tombs — known locally as The Hill Of The Witch — near Oldcastle, Meath, where more than 30 mounds are grouped together. No decent records were kept of the items taken, which presumably are now in private collections somewhere. But at least those responsible didn't remove a crude stone basin, probably used for rituals, neither could they take the large stones decorated with Neolithic art — U-shapes, sun symbols, snakes, spirals, 'fishbone' lines and zig-zags.

Fortunately for today's archaeologists the three great passage tomb clusters of Meath's Boyne Valley, namely Newgrange, Knowth and Dowth were not subject to similar raids and have produced numerous important finds. One of these was the Knowth mace head, a superb ceremonial implement carved from flint and mounted on a wooden handle.

Before leaving passage tombs it is worth mentioning Newgrange's hallowed place in Irish folklore. According to the early analysts it was both the final resting place of the kings of Tara (more of which later) and entrance to an underworld populated by the supernatural Tuatha de Danainn (people of the goddess Danu). Newgrange was also said to have been the home of the god Dagda and his son Oengus.

• Wedge Tombs: These are Ireland's most common megalithic monument, with almost 400 located — mostly west of a line between Cork and Derry. The rectangular shaped burial chamber was often higher towards the front and roofed with large stones which were encased in a wedge-shaped earthwork mound. Wedge tombs are thought to be the later megaliths and may have been the work of Bronze Age man after 2000AD. Some have suggested they were designed by a 'new wave' of colonists from France, who landed in southern Ireland and spread their influence north and west. Among the most interesting are those of Baurnadomeeny, Co Tipperary, Labbacallee, Co Cork, Ballyedmonduff, Co Dublin, and Moytirra, Co Sligo. Moytirra excavations have produced some of the best examples of 'beaker' pottery in all Ireland.

The precise social and religious significance of the four different types of tombs is still largely guesswork. There was almost certainly a belief in the spirit world and it is possible that keeping an ancestor's bones in the village where he lived was a way of laying down land rights. Whatever the truth, the tombs were not the only sacred sites. Stone circles, of which there are around 200 in Ireland (mostly in the south-west and Ulster), must surely have hosted religious gatherings — perhaps for the worship of the sun and stars or to pay homage to pagan nature gods. The purpose of standing stones, prevalent almost everywhere in Ireland, is less clear. Some appear to form alignments with the more important circles, while others might have been markers for ancient trackways or gravestones.

One of the most elaborate circles is at Grange, in Co. Limerick, where the prehistoric builders erected stones up to 2.7m (9ft) tall. Grange is surrounded by a large earthen bank with a clear entranceway on the eastern side. The land within the stones was originally floored with clay, raising it about 61cm (2ft) above that outside, and it clearly held great significance for those who used it. But the assertion that Grange, and similar circles in Cork and Kerry, were sophisticated lunar observatories is debatable. There is some small evidence that stones were set to correspond to a point on the skyline marking the rise or fall of the sun, moon and stars. Why though, if this were all that was needed, did the Neolithic builders not rely simply on two key stones to make an alignment? At the moment all we can say with certainty is that the movement of celestial bodies influenced the siting of circles and standing stones. Dromberg circle in Co Cork, for instance, is set up along the line of the winter solstice sunset.

Whenever prehistoric stone circles are discussed, there is inevitably speculation about the use of some form of sacrifice by the religious leaders of the day. A combination of ancient mythology, folklore and over-imaginative film scripts have today conjured up images of men in white cloaks and hoods cutting the throat of some terrified virgin tied to a sacrificial stone. Such scenarios seem unlikely, but it would be wrong to pretend human sacrifice did not happen. One henge-type circle on the moor at Curragh in Co Kildare has a central grave in which was found the remains of a young woman. The position of the skeleton is highly unusual and does suggest that she was buried alive. The head was probably upright,

one hand and one leg were pressed against the side of the grave and the legs were apart. A few miles from this site, though probably unconnected, we find the Punchestown standing stone which, at 6.4m (21ft), is the tallest in Ireland.

Outside Cork and Kerry, the Ulster stone circles are the most dramatic. Particularly noteworthy is the Beaghmore cluster near Cookstown, Co Tyrone where three pairs of circles and a single one studded with 884 small boulders have been built within a few hundred metres of each other. The site also contains numerous cairns and standing stones but the reasons behind its layout are unknown. One academic has speculated that a line of four stones nearby could have been used to pinpoint the rising moon on the horizon in about 1640BC.

Finally, we come to the other intriguing aspect of prehistoric architecture — a trend which probably followed the wedge tombs and stone circles — the stone rows. In Ireland the vast majority of these were short, comprising only three to six stones, but there were many more of them than in England, Scotland and Brittany. There are around 30 four-to-six stone rows, nearly 60 three-stone rows and well over a 100 stone pairs. The short rows seem to be independent of circles or tombs and are much more common in the south and west. Ulster has a dense concentration of both long and short rows.

Extensive research by the archaeologist Ann Lynch in southwest Ireland has proved conclusive links to astronomical alignments. Of the 37 short rows she plotted, 23 showed significant alignments to the solstices and/or the major extremes of the moon. But this does not necessarily imply that Neolithic or Bronze Age astronomers had an advanced scientific understanding. These were people who spent much of their lives staring at the night sky and the movements of the sun, moon, stars and planets would have evoked far more general interest, and undoubtedly far more significance, among the population than they do today. The stone rows may simply have been an aid to observation, and therefore to the timing of rituals and festivals.

The emergence of the Irish rows seems to have coincided with exploitation of the first copper mines. Irish copper and Cornish tin combined made bronze, and the start of the Bronze Age in Ireland (from roughly 2000BC) must have seen an eruption in trading links between these two lands and Brittany — another major outlet for bronze items. One offshoot of this trade would have been an exchange of ideas and the Bretons, who built Europe's most impressive stone row complex at Carnac, may well have exported their beliefs to the Irish and Cornish. It was the dawn of a new era, a time in which metalworking was the growth industry. For Ireland, it was the beginning of a golden age.

Previous Page: *A neolithic dual-court chambered tomb, circa 2000BC, at Ballyreagh near Tempo.*

Opposite above: *The massive capstone of the Browneshill portal tomb, Co Carlow, is thought to weigh more than 100 tons.*

Opposite below: *The Carrowkeel passage tombs in Co Sligo form one of Ireland's most important early cemeteries.*

Above: *Another view of the partially-collapsed Browneshill dolmen.*

Left: *A decorated stone from the great tomb complex at Knowth, in the Boyne valley, Co Meath. This form of prehistoric art is more common in the east of the country.*

Opposite: *The Burren, Co Clare, has numerous examples of Ireland's commonest megalith — the wedge tomb.*

Above: *Beneath a threatening Irish sky, the graves at Carrowkeel have a truly atmospheric quality.*

Left: *The Neolithic settlement at Lough Gur, Co Limerick, (now reconstructed) has yielded important clues to the spread of 'Beaker' pottery in the north of Ireland.*

Opposite: *Ireland's tallest standing stone at Punchestown, Co. Kildare, stands more than 6.5m (21ft) high.*

Above: *A general view of the Knowth passage grave complex. It ranks alongside the temples of Malta as prehistoric Europe's greatest monumental architecture.*

Left: *The Catstone megaliths of West Meath.*

Opposite above: *A view through the remains of Creevykeel Court Cairn, Co Sligo. It is more than 61m (200ft) long and has an entrance 'court' measuring 15 by 9m (50 by 30ft).*

Opposite below: *Stone circles such as this one at Carrowmore may have combined religious, social and scientific purposes.*

Above: *The impressive stonework forming the roof of Newgrange, Co Meath is easily Ireland's best known megalithic monument. Conservative estimates suggest that Newgrange, which is orientated to the mid-winter sunrise, may have taken 30 years to build.*

Left: *The squat Aghnacliff dolmen in Co Longford.*

Opposite: *Another stone circle from the Carrowmore cemetery in Co Sligo. The site's religious significance may date from as early as the 4th millennium BC.*

Above: *The purpose of these standing stones at Oran, Co Roscommon remains a mystery.*

Right: *Hundreds of visitors every year come to view the Creevykeel court cairn.*

Opposite above: *One of Ireland's largest stone circles is the Grange, in the Lough Gur area of Co Limerick. The area within the circle was raised by an 45cm (18in) deep clay floor.*

Opposite below: *Another view of the Grange stones.*

Derrintaggart stone circle stands on the Beara Peninsula, Co. Cork.

BURIED TREASURE FROM A GOLDEN AGE

The discovery of copper sometime after 2000BC heralded the start of an Irish metalworking industry which became renowned in western Europe. In archaeological terms this was more accurately the beginning of the Bronze Age, a time of new technology for the prehistoric Irish and the arrival of many economic changes. The country's copper mining centre was Cork and Kerry and it is thought they together produced a remarkable 375,920kg (370 tons) of finished copper. Given that the total number of pre-1400BC copper and bronze objects discovered in Ireland amounts to little over 748kg (1,650lb), the Irish must have built up a healthy export trade. It is difficult to imagine all that metal being lost in the soil or melted down for a fast buck by succeeding generations.

Digging out copper was a hard life. The miners would cut a passage downwards into the copper vein and then enlarge it into a small, rocky room. They would heat water on an underground fire (this depended heavily on the oxygen available) and throw it onto the surrounding walls to shatter the ore-bearing rock. They would then scrape off the ore using rough pebbles fastened to their hands by rope. This Cork and Kerry copper industry left behind the only known examples of prehistoric mines in Europe, outside Austria. There are at least 25 mine shafts clustered together on Mount Gabriel, near Schull, Co Cork, although flooding has prevented all but two from being properly explored. They seem to date from between 1500BC and 1180BC.

Copper quickly become a status symbol. Ownership of a mine would give a family both kudos and wealth and there must have been many prospecting parties dispatched to find the tell-tale traces of green malachite and blue azurite in rocky areas of the countryside. Bronze (a mixture of copper and tin) and gold also emerged at this time and quickly became sought after. A bronze dagger or axe head was far superior in its strength and cutting edge to stone. Furthermore, the metal was easily worked — it would be poured molten into a stone mould, cooled and hammered into shape — and could be 'customised' with magical symbols to impress both its owner and his enemy!

Irish bronze metalworking reached a high point early in the Bronze Age. Metal axe production then fell quite dramatically (the reasons are unclear) and there seemed to be a tendency for the original Irish styles to be dropped in favour of longer weapons with curving blades. These were probably modelled on English designs, which in turn copied continental fashions. Gradually new weapons became widely available — the spearhead, the rapier and, by around 800BC, the sword. While the southern Mediterranean's Bronze Age chiefs were being engulfed by waves of central European barbarians, the west was left alone to develop its own distinctive bronze and gold industry. For Ireland it was the apex of a Golden Age.

Intriguingly, as well as producing vast quantities of metalware the Irish were very keen on burying it. Numerous treasure troves have been dated to this era and there must have been a number of reasons why concealment was so important. The obvious one is that wealthy families and metalsmiths took precautions to protect their assets during times of war or unrest. But there might also have been a religious aspect. Many of the hoards have been discovered in rivers, marshes and other sites close to water. Perhaps the Bronze Age was a time of climatic change in western Europe and rain was either in short supply or too prevalent. Were the treasure hoards ritual offerings aimed at calming the wrath of some nature god? If so, the owners were happy to donate in large quantities. Hoards such as the Dowris, found between two lakes in Co Offaly during the early 19th century, amounted to more than 200 items.

Among these were five swords, leaf-shaped spearheads, numerous axe heads, gouges, chisels, knives and instruments which may have been razors. There were also 'crotals', thought by some to be weights used in trading but by others to be modelled on bulls' scrotums and made to the specifications of a European fertility cult. In support of this second theory there were also 26 bronze horns, each skilfully cast in two separate pieces; these were undoubtedly modelled on bulls horns.

Most interesting of all was the Dowris 'bucket' made of decorated bronze sheets, which was imported from central Europe sometime after the 8th century BC. This may well have been an important vessel for religious ritual, along with a cauldron found nearby. In early Irish mythology cauldrons played a critical role in appeasing the gods — particularly Dagda, the god of health and plenty. It is not difficult to imagine the meat-filled Dowris cauldron being carried in to an open-air ritual feast, its arrival heralded by the horn-players.

Gold hoards are also relatively common in Ireland and in them lies confirmation of the country's lofty status as a major European goldwork producer. The quality of the materials, and degree of craftsmanship, matches or exceeds any other Late Bronze Age society. Irish ornaments were surely highly prized throughout the ancient world.

Opposite above: *A golden collar, part of the hoard found at Broighter, Co Derry, and now held by the National Museum of Ireland in Dublin. Ornaments such as this, and the torc* **(Opposite below)***, were highly-prized among the jewellery-loving Celts. As metalworking techniques improved, La Tene artwork flourished across the land.*

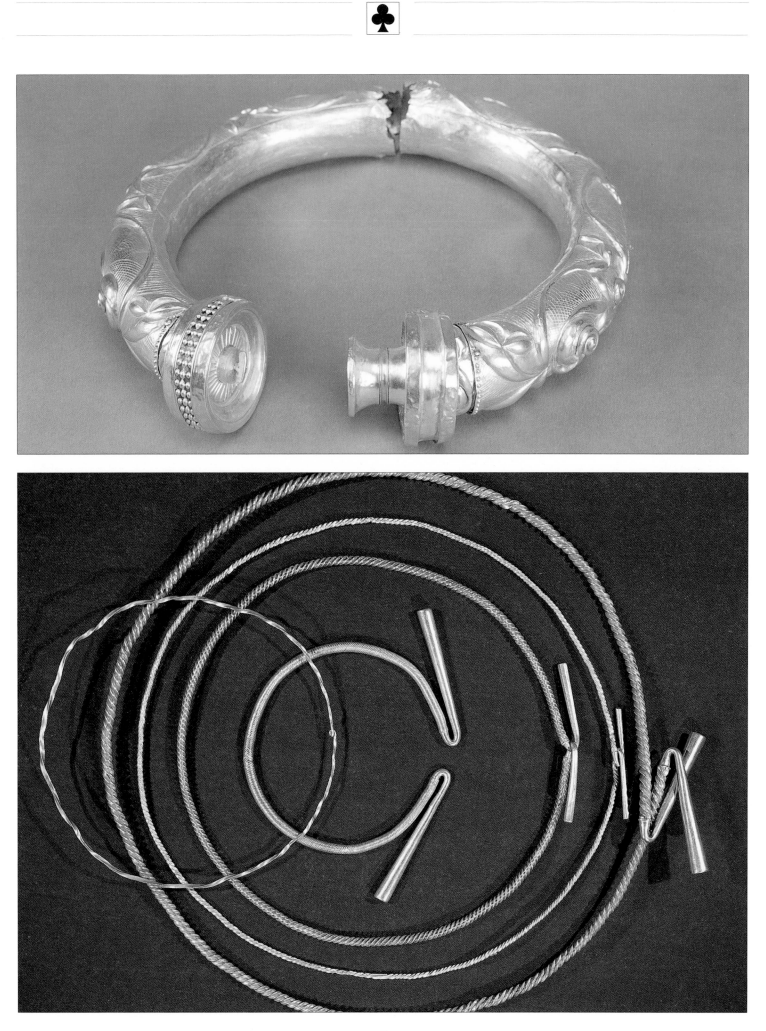

The most dazzling hoard so far discovered is the 'Great Clare Find' of 1854, when 146 objects were dug up close to the Mooghaun North hill fort, Co Clare. The treasure was discovered by a construction gang working on tracks for the West Clare narrow-gauge railway. It is believed to be the largest single discovery of gold Bronze Age pieces outside the Aegean. Unfortunately much of it was melted down for hard cash, though not before casts were made (these are now in the care of the National Museum at Dublin). The priceless hoard included golden collars, neck-rings, bracelets and cloak-fasteners.

At least two other noteworthy Clare hoards have been found — at Gorteenreagh and at Gleninsheen. Gorteenreagh threw up an ornamental 'lock ring' which, it is thought, was used as a hair decoration. At first glance the ring appears to have been decorated with very fine concentric scratches. But under a microscope these 'scratches' appear as tiny strands of wire, less than a third of a millimetre thick. Few jewellers today could make the wire, let alone fit it onto the ring.

The location of these Irish gold mines is tantalising; the Wicklow Hills were certainly a rich source, although by no means the only one. It is likely that the Sperrin Mountains, in Co Tyrone, contained some veins and many of the rivers probably washed down more gold than they do today. It seems unlikely that the smiths ever needed to import their raw materials, which in any case would have been an expensive and hazardous task.

All counties bordering the River Shannon estuary and its lower reaches seem to have had a tradition of gold-making (judging by the number of ornaments that turn up). One explanation is that it was a convenient place from which to export; another is that foreign goldsmiths arrived by ship there and decided to stick around. Either way, influences from abroad clearly impressed the Irish and elements of German and Scandinavian designs began to creep into their work. There also seems to have been a trading link from the southern Mediterranean, across southern France and up the western seaboard of Europe. Irish gold ornaments would be exchanged for spearheads, swords and new axe designs, as well as more mundane products.

In terms of its standing in Western Europe, Ireland was relatively richer in the Late Bronze Age that it has ever been — either before or since. A strong indication of this is the way economic prosperity set off a huge expansion in farming. Pollen samples from around 800BC show the land was largely heath, bog, bracken and peat. Yet by 400BC large tracts had been re-claimed as grassland or for the planting of grain. The great irony for the Irish today is that so little else is known about this period in their history. We have hazy theories on religious beliefs, absolutely no clue as to the political and military situation and a dearth of reliable evidence about family life. The hopes and fears of Ireland's late Bronze Age remain an enigma and we can only hope that some still-to-be-discovered settlement will bring further enlightenment.

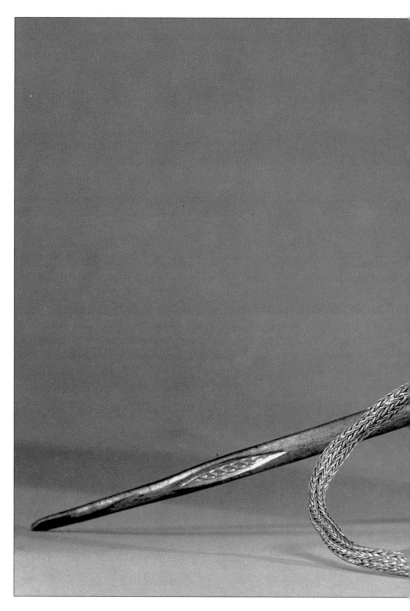

Above: *The fabulous Tara brooch, a potent symbol of Ireland's Celtic heritage. The 8th century brooch, discovered at Bettystown, Co Meath, is fashioned from gold, silver, copper, glass, enamel and amber.*

Opposite: *The economic importance of the River Shannon estuary was rooted in its Celtic metalworking industry. Later, fortifications such as this sprang up along its banks.*

ROMANS IN IRELAND

For years historians remained convinced that Ireland had escaped the Roman conquest of Europe. There was so little evidence of any permanent settlement; no sign of a fort or even of a temporary camp. The bits and bobs of Roman relics which turned up were explained away merely as imports brought in by travellers and traders. Ireland was seen as some kind of heroic twilight of the Celtic peoples, defying the march of the legions in a way Britain had failed to match. Then, in the mid 1980s, this 'official' version of history began to fall apart.

Gradually word spread among the country's leading archaeologists of a newly discovered site at Drumanagh, 24km (15 miles) north of Dublin. At first it was considered to be only a small encampment, the temporary home of a Roman expeditionary force sent to discover what lay beyond the western seas of Britain. But as time went on, and more fieldwork was carried out, the extraordinary truth began to emerge. A small group of archaeologists was granted access under conditions of strict secrecy. The National Museum of Ireland took possession of several valuable Roman items but decided not to put them on display. The concern was that treasure-hunters armed with metal detectors would descend on the site in their droves and plunder the evidence.

It was not until January 1996 that the true scale of the Roman settlement was revealed. Drumanagh appears to have been a massive Roman coastal fort which must have housed hundreds if not thousands of people. The 1,618sq m (40 acre) site was probably a beachhead constructed to support Roman armies on campaign in Ireland during the 1st and 2nd centuries AD. The first coins discovered bear the names of the emperors Titus, Trajan and Hadrian, which indicates a Roman presence at least between 79 and 138AD. Later the fort seems to have developed into an important trading post.

The Drumanagh excavation is likely to prove the most important in the history of Ireland. Archaeologists believe it fits in perfectly with Roman activities along every frontier in the empire and it will certainly help explain the widespread scatter of Roman artifacts already dug up across Ireland. Although nothing is yet certain, it seems Drumanagh helped establish a considerable Roman influence across much of the country's east coast. One discovery which supports this is the grave of a Romano-British warrior chief on Lambay Island, 4.8km (3 miles) off shore. Another is the theory that for many years the Romans tried to interfere in Ireland's internal politics by re-establishing kingdoms for Irish noblemen exiled in Britain.

Among these exiles was the late 1st century chieftain Tuathal Techtmar, who is thought to have tried to reclaim his lands with the aid of a Roman-trained and equipped mercenary army. Another, separate, Roman-backed campaign may have led to the founding of Cashel, an important ancient town in Tipperary whose name is derived from the Latin word *Castellum*. During the nin-

Above: *Ogham Stones such as this one at Kilmalkedar, Co Kerry, carried the first Irish writing — believed to have been inspired by contact with Roman numerals.*

Opposite: *One of Ireland's most distinctive castles is the Rock of Cashel, Co Tipperary. There is thought to have been a fortress here since Roman times.*

teenth century fragments of surgical equipment belonging to a Roman eye surgeon were discovered in Tipperary but it was so out of keeping with the area's known history that it was dismissed as a freak find. Now it seems the surgeon's tools, along with just about every other Roman find in Ireland, will have to be carefully reassessed.

THE COMING
OF THE CELTS

Of all the foreigners who settled in Ireland, none left a cultural legacy to rival the Celts. They were proud and resourceful, brave and intelligent and they established a way of life and language that persists even today. It was the Celts who first defended Irish soil from invaders during the Viking Wars, and they mounted the first Irish attacks on foreign soil (their raids on western Britain during the 3rd and 4th centuries AD).

Yet there is absolutely no evidence that the Celts colonised Ireland through some massive invasion force. Their arrival was gradual — over hundreds if not thousands of years — and their customs and skills became ingrained rather than imposed. For all the fearsome raiding of the Norsemen and the brutally efficient Norman armies, it was the Celts who really shaped the Irish society we know today.

But who were the Celts and where did they come from? To answer this we have to look to the heart of Europe around 500BC.

Writers at this time began making references to a barbaric, illiterate, warlike race who occupied much of the Alpine region along with parts of central France and Spain. They were named the Keltoi by the Greeks and the Celtae by the Romans, although there was no suggestion that they had their own empire. True, the Celts shared a religious heritage and a broadly common language but there were also major differences between the tribes. The political order would range from large regional Celtic governments to kings commanding little more than a few settlements. In addition and contrary to popular opinion, they were by no means all followers of the Druids.

The Celts had obviously been around for many hundreds of years before they were 'recognised' by the annalists. Celtic speakers probably occupied pockets of land throughout Europe (including Ireland) early in the Bronze Age and continued migration would have established them further and further north and west. But it was the rise of the so-called La Téne Celts in the 5th century that really grabbed the attention of Greek and Roman political and military leaders.

La Téne Celts get their name from a distinctive style of highly decorative art — on metalwork, pottery, graves and in settlements. The name comes from a site in Switzerland where, in the mid-19th century, archaeologists discovered some extraordinary Celtic treasures. The La Téne designs which flourished in centres like these would dominate British and Irish artwork for well over 1,000 years.

But in 400BC it was not La Téne culture that concerned the Romans and the Greeks. A number of large, powerful tribes had begun storming across the Alps and into northern Italy. Some settled in the Po Valley, attacking and plundering Rome around 390BC. Others moved east into Greece and it is thought they may have sacked Delphi in 279BC. That was the end of the Celts colonial history. From the 2nd century on, the all-powerful Roman Empire flexed its muscles, conquering their lands and imposing an entirely new law and language. As the Romans moved inexorably across western Europe, the La Téne Celts found themselves forced to adapt. Only the fringes of the Roman Empire — Scotland, Wales, western England, Brittany, the Isle of Man and parts of Ireland — were left in relative peace to develop in their own distinctive ways. It is no accident that today these sanctuaries remain the only places where the Celtic language is still spoken; that it has survived at all is largely thanks to pressures from nationalist groups in the areas concerned.

Unravelling Ireland's Celtic past is, in many ways, just as difficult as tackling its Bronze or Stone Age periods. For one thing, the Celts left no records of their own. For another, it is almost impossible to be sure how widespread they were at any one time. Very often all we are left with are the tainted or fictionalised writings of later historians.

The celebrated Greek geographer Strabo, who lived around the time of the birth of Christ, was only too well aware of this. In his *Geography of the Ancient World* he writes of Ireland: 'Concerning this island I have nothing certain to tell, except that its inhabitants are more savage than the Britons, since they are man-eaters as well as heavy eaters, and since, further, they count it an honourable thing, when their fathers die, to devour them, and openly to have intercourse, not only with the other women, but also with their mothers and sisters.' Strabo knew that the travellers' tales he'd heard were likely to have been embellished and he went on to warn his readers: 'I am saying this only with the understanding that I have no trustworthy witnesses for it...'

According to the much later *Book of Invasions* which medieval scholars argued that pre-Christian Ireland had been conquered by waves of intrepid invaders, the country's founding fathers were apparently Celts and a people called the Fír Bolg. While these shadowy groups bear similarities to Gaelic tribes living in France and Belgium, there is no clear evidence of any 'invasion'.

Despite the absence of hard facts, it has been possible to draw some conclusions on the lives of the Celts in Ireland. These ideas

Opposite above: *Part of the stone fortifications at the Grianan Aileagh hillfort in Co Donegal. Here Celtic architects created a large, stone wall as a central defensive point within a number of earth ramparts.*

Opposite below: *Prehistoric stonework displayed in the National Heritage Park at Ferrycarrig, Co Wexford.*

are based partly on Greek and Roman historians, partly on surviving language and place names and partly on archaeological analysis of settlements, land use, excavations of forts, farms and tombs, weapons and tools and the skeletons of the people themselves. Archaeology is very far from being an exact science but at least it has given us a few clues.

Celtic society in Ireland was a haphazard collection of family tribes, each ruled by a king. These tribes would occasionally come together (perhaps for a counsel of war) to strike deals and form political alliances. But Celtic politics was a precarious business and there was no sense of any national identity.

Within the tribe, the pecking order was clearer. Beneath the king would come the warrior nobility, followed by those considered to have special skills — Druid priests, storytellers, artists, craftsman and seers. Among the early Celts the king would have had strictly limited powers and any important decisions would have been taken by vote of all free men in the tribe. This semi-democracy seems to have broken down in later years with tribal leaders becoming more autocratic.

One easy way of judging the importance of a king was to cast an eye over his jewellery. The Celts could not get enough trinkets and they held a significance way beyond fashion or petty vanities. Jewellery conveyed a person's wealth and standing in society, it could be imbued with magical symbols and it served as an heirloom to assist with the tangible handing down of power. Brooches, bracelets and anklets of enamelled bronze, necklets (particularly copper, iron or gold torcs), elaborately crafted bronze chains and ornate belts were all much in vogue. Jewellery was worn as much by men as by women and certain styles may have been emblems of rank, age or authority.

Political life was male-dominated, although occasionally noblewomen such as Connacht's Queen Maeve took very prominent positions. The best known example of a powerful female leader however emerged across the water in Celtic Britain where Boudicca, Queen of the Iceni, massacred around 70,000 Romans before her revolt was ruthlessly crushed. The historian Cassius Dio said of her: 'In stature she was very tall, in appearance most terrifying, in the glance of her eye most fierce, and her voice was harsh; a great mass of the tawniest hair fell to her hips; around her neck was a large golden necklace; and she wore a tunic of diverse colours over which a thick mantle was fastened with a brooch. This was her invariable attire. She now grasped a spear to aid her in terrifying all beholders and spoke...'

Celtic women shared their menfolk's sense of pride along with a determination to avenge personal insult. When Chiomara, wife of the Galatian leader Ortiagon, was captured, enslaved and raped she persuaded the Roman centurion who had violated her that she could be ransomed. A deal was struck, the ransom was brought to a secret meeting place and the gleeful centurion walked away with his ill-gotten gains. Hardly had he turned his back when she ordered her kinsmen to slaughter him. She then cut off his head and presented it to her husband. 'Woman, a fine thing is good faith', scolded Ortiagon. 'A better thing only one man should be alive who had sex with me,' she replied.

Chiomara's sense of chastity aside, the Celts were a people of moral contradictions. On the one hand there are signs that women participated in sex with a number of different partners, and that noblemen had several wives. On the other, many Celtic marriages seem to have been solemn affairs in which both sides pooled equal amounts of wealth and pledged fidelity and respect to the other. The idea that men had power to legally murder their wives now seems to be more fable than fact.

Feasting and drinking were fundamental rituals of life and as trade routes developed with the Mediterranean demand for wine grew inexorably. Wine would be served up in large quantities, as much a status symbol as proof of generosity, and allowed a king to emphasise his wealth and authority over the subordinate nobles sitting in order of importance down the table.

One curious aspect of Celtic feasting was the presence of a 'praise poet', a bard who would recite sycophantic songs and poems extolling the great deeds of the leading warriors and, of course, the king. Interestingly, there would often be a satirist (a kind of court jester) as well. He would direct jibes at some of the inflated egos around him and was a much feared face at the table. In a society where pride and image was everything, the voice was indeed sometimes mightier than the sword.

If feasts were ritualistic, war was even more so. Celtic armies were very often alliances of different tribes and on the battlefield these tribes would march and fight together. Each would have its own standard — usually an animal figure — which served as a rallying point for re-grouping. The standard often had its own religious significance and fighters would bow down to it, convinced of its magical powers.

Where two armies met, the actual fighting could be delayed by several hours while a bizarre display of rituals was performed. Sometimes champions from either side would face each other in single combat, boasting loudly of their past victories, their bravery, their skills and their great ancestry. Once this charade was over a psychological war would begin with flamboyant false charges and spectacular rapid movements by charioteers and infantrymen. Above it all a war chant would strike up, backed by the sound of sword on shield and swelled by the haunting sound of the battle horn. In this way the Celts hoped to un-nerve their opponents and in this they were no doubt very often successful. Only in continental Europe, where the Celts found themselves up against highly disciplined, well-trained Roman legionnaires, did the tactic tend to founder.

By around 200BC the Iron Age in Ireland was becoming well established. The use of iron meant lighter, stronger weapons, tools and chariots — factors which must have had far-reaching military and social effects. It is hard to say exactly when the Celts began to work iron, but it was certainly not an overnight revolution. The likeliest scenario is that iron began to emerge way back in the Bronze Age, perhaps as early as the 6th or 7th century BC, and gradually gained acceptance among the smiths. Even when its use was widespread it did not totally replace bronze, which remained popular in jewellery and for the decoration of horses and chariots.

The Celts religious beliefs remain a mystery to us today, mainly because nothing was ever written down. Their priests were often Druids (there were a few other holy sects such as the Vates) and there can be few faiths throughout history which operated with such obsessive secrecy. This of course helped the Druids defend their power base in Celtic society. Because they were so secretive

Opposite: *Excavations at the Drombeg stone circle, Co Cork, revealed a flat-bottomed pot containing cremated human remains. It had been intentionally broken before it was buried.*

they were feared, and because they were feared their views carried great influence. The fact that so many novices were picked from the ranks of the nobility was a further prop to their authority.

It seems the roots of Druidism were in Britain. Caesar tells how the novice priests of western Europe were sent there because the country had a reputation for offering the most thorough induction training. However, the legendary meeting place of the Druids was in Gaul. The priests, for whom the oak was a sacred symbol of 'earth power', were said to congregate in an oak forest somewhere in the Carnutes tribal area each year, when they would elect a Chief Druid. This chief would hold sway over all priests and tribal loyalties had to be cast aside in deference to him.

Despite their shadowy reputation, priests were familiar faces in any settlement and would mix and talk with their kinsmen quite freely. They were dowsers and healers, as well as the teachers, judges and guardians of tribal history. They had the power to mete out punishments, such as excommunicating tribesmen from sacrificial gatherings. They were both prophets and personal advisers — suggesting 'lucky days' on which to do important business. They acted as mediators between ordinary mortals and the gods.

Druids supervised the training of priests (this could take up to 20 years because all Druid philosophy was committed to memory and novices had to learn long tracts of law, verse, history and magic formulae). They organised the calendar (one reason for the astronomical connections with prehistoric stone circles) and, although they were themselves excused military duties, they helped draft treaties and negotiate peace. When the time came for a Druid meeting, or the enactment of magic, they would cut themselves off from outsiders. For many ordinary mortals the only sight of a Druid in his religious cloak and hood would come with the performance of a sacrifice.

The frequency and method of human sacrifice in Ireland is an area easily distorted by events on the continent. There is little doubt that the Druids in Gaul and central Europe inflicted the most hideous ritual murders on both their kinsfolk and their enemies. There are stories of giant wooden cages, filled with straw, people and animals, being set alight. Of sacrificial victims being hurled into deep pits to die a lonely, lingering death. Of men being stabbed in the back to allow dispassionate Druid seers to foretell the future from their death throes. Of prisoners-of-war being forced over ritual cauldrons to have their throats cut; and even of volunteers for sacrifice, whose duty was to bear important messages to the gods.

Whatever the exaggerations of early historians, both animal and human sacrifice was an indisputable part of the Druid way. One 'sanctuary' of the Gauls at Ribemont-sur-Ancre has revealed the bodies of at least 1,000 people, aged between 15 and 40, many of whom had been ritually decapitated and dismembered. The fact that these activities happened on the continent does not automatically mean that they occurred in Ireland. But, given the free exchange of ideas between Celts and Druids of different countries, the chances are that some form of human sacrifice was practiced.

The main purpose of these gruesome rituals was to appease the wrath of the gods. They were closely linked to the four main Celtic religious festivals — Imbole (1 February), linked with Brigid the Irish goddess of childbirth, Beltain (1 May), linked to sun worship and fertility, Lughnasa (1 August), the harvest festival, and Samhain (1 November), the start of the Celtic year and the day barriers to the underworld were lifted. Samhain is still celebrated in many parts of the world today as Hallowe'en, a contraction of 'All Hallows Eve'.

No book about ancient Ireland can be complete without some mention of the country's treasure chest of Celtic myth and legend. Many of these began as folk stories, surviving in verbal form from generation to generation, but later they were carefully written down by the monks. The most famous is the Ulster Cycle featuring an epic story called the *Tàin Bo Cúailnge* (Cattle Raid of Cooley). This is the Irish equivalent of England's King Arthur or Scandinavia's Beowulf and recounts the heroic deeds of Ulster's King Conchobar mac Nessa and his circle of warrior chiefs and noblewomen. The greatest of these fighters was Cú Chulainn (Hound of Culann) and the amazing magical powers he possesses.

The Tàin is made up of many different tales with extravagant titles such as *The Tooth Fight of Fintain, The Bloodless Fight of Rochad* and *The Missile Throwing of the Charioteers*. It is impossible to do it justice with brief extracts but the story of how the Hound of Culann got his name at least gives a flavour of the epic. The story below is an abridged paraphrase.

One day the smith Culann made ready a feast for Conchobar, king of Ulster, and sent word asking the king to travel with only a few companions, since his smithy did not provide a good enough living to feed a large host. Conchobar therefore decided to bring along just 50 of his bravest knights. As the journey began, the King noticed a young boy fostered at his palace playing against 150 others. The boy defeated each of them with ease in ball games and at wrestling and soon the king called him over to invite him to the feast. The boy replied: 'Master Conchobar, I have not yet finished playing but I shall follow you later on.'

When Conchobar arrived at the feast Culann asked if anyone else was following. The king had already forgotten the young boy and said 'no'. Culann then unleashed his giant, ferocious hound to guard the approaches to his fortified home. But at that very moment the boy came into sight and the hound sprang to savage him. Untroubled, the boy cast down his ball and hurley, grabbed the hound with his bare hands and dashed it to death upon a stone.

The Ulstermen ran to the boy and took him back to Conchobar. The king was greatly relieved, for he now discovered that the child was Sédanta mac Sualtamh, son of his sister. Remembering his duties as host, Culann welcomed the boy but mourned the death of his dog for it had given loyal service in defence of his property. The boy replied: 'I shall raise a puppy of the same breed for you and until he is ready to serve you I shall protect you and your cattle myself.' Cathbad the Druid then stepped forward and told the youth: 'Then you shall be called the Hound of Culann (Cú Chulainn)'.

Right: *Settled in pre-Christian times, Lower Lough Erne contains many islands. In the Romanesque church on White Island stand enigmatic statues of Celtic saints, they are probably from the remains of an earlier monastery dating from around the 9th-10th century.*

This Page and Opposite: *Lower Lough Erne stretches for 18 miles from Enniskillen to Belleek. Its islands and shores are scattered with religious sites and buildings: none more so than White Island in Castle Archdale Bay. There, built into the wall of the Romanesque church, are enigmatic figures. They look pagan but they probably decorated an earlier monastery.*

THE DAWN OF CHRISTIANITY

No one knows for sure when the first Christian missionaries set foot in Ireland, but it was probably around the 4th or 5th century AD. The first mention of an Irish Church was recorded by Prosper Tiro, one of Europe's leading opponents of a 'heretic' version of Christianity called Pelagianism. Its founder, Pelagius, who lived at the end of the 4th century, rejected the idea of man's original sin and convinced his followers that everyone had an in-built desire to do good. Pelagian heresy had spread through Ireland by the time Pope Celestine sent his French deacon Palladius to stamp it out in 431AD. Prosper writes that Palladius was sent as bishop to 'the Irish who believe in Christ', a reference to all who followed the orthodox teaching.

The conversion of Ireland to Christianity was a slow process and many people still regard St Patrick, a Briton, as the man who takes most of the credit. In fact, there were many Christian settlements in the country before his mission took place sometime around the middle of the 5th century. Patrick's legacy was that he probably endured more hardship and danger than any previous Irish missionary and took his faith into areas which had remained firmly pagan. The fact that it was a time of great change — the Western Roman Empire was falling apart — perhaps helped him. His teachings seemed to offer certainty in an uncertain world.

Sadly, very little is known about Patrick himself, apart from the few snippets gleaned from his own writings. He seems to have been born in western Britain and was called either Magonus, Succetus or, later on, by the Roman name Patricius. His father was a church deacon who doubled as a local government official and the family was therefore relatively wealthy. It was most likely their country estate which singled them out as a target for the Irish raiders who at that time were pillaging Britain's western seaboard.

The 16-year-old Patrick was captured and taken to Ireland as a slave. For six years he lived in the north Connacht area herding sheep but eventually escaped, walked 320km (200 miles) begging what food he could, and obtained passage back to Britain aboard a pagan-crewed ship. A love of the Irish was clearly instilled in him however for he returned later to preach the gospel. Patrick emphasises that he was by then a bishop, although it is unlikely he was sent with the Church's blessing. He seems to have been criticised by his peers as unsuitable to tackle the heathen Irish.

Patrick's stronghold became Armagh, where his local followers worked hard to foster his emergence as a saint. The town established itself as one of the most important Christian outposts of western Europe and by the 7th century Patrick's teachings had spread throughout the north-east of Ireland and into Munster.

However, the organisation of the early church was haphazard, so the organised church evolved through a number of different branches. When the first great monasteries began to spring up in the 6th century they did not claim any link to St Patrick. Instead

Above: A masonry arch at the Rock of Cashel. The fortress was handed over to the Church in 1101.

Opposite: The early Christian stonemasons afforded lavish attention to detail, as seen on Kells High Cross, Co Meath.

monastic leaders such as Columba, Finian of Clonard, Ciarán of Clonmacnoise, and Brendan of Clonfert were heavily influenced by the British church. From humble beginnings as places of retreat and personal discipline they soon attracted the interest of wealthy noblemen and became influential in their own right. This form of patronage allowed literacy and the arts to flourish. A new form of art — called Hiberno-Saxon — blended the styles of the Irish, the Anglo-Saxons and the Picts and among the best-known examples is the magnificent 'Tara' brooch, dug up at Bettystone, Co Meath. Dating from the 8th century it was fashioned from gold, silver. copper, glass, enamel and amber.

The earliest Irish writing is thought to be Ogham, a system in which straight lines were cut along the edge of wood or stone. Ogham probably began to appear around the 4th century AD as Irish scholars became more familiar with Latin and Roman numerals. Ogham stones were raised across southern Ireland and the extreme west of Britain (where the Irish settled). But by the late 7th century literacy had become rather more refined as a result of monasteries turning out many Latin-trained scholars. These were men with a thorough grounding in Biblical doctrine. They used Christian tenets as a basis for common law and so began to construct the first building blocks of a civilised society.

This page and Opposite: *Skellig Michael, also known as Great Skellig, is an inhospitable and austere pinnacle of rock jutting out of the Atlantic, upon which for 5-600 years a small monastery existed consisting of six corbelled beehive cells and two boat-shaped oratories. The monks remained on this bleak island through-out the 12th century, until they retreated to the Augustinian priory at Ballinskellig on the mainland.*

Within the Church and the Christian land-owning classes this task was fairly straightforward. The *Collectio Canonum Hibernensis* of around 700AD set out the principles of internal church law, property ownership, wills, government, marriage and right of sanctuary. But among the wider population, where a belief in paganism and 'earth magic' was still rife, the church faced a much tougher mission. They got round the problem by assuring the masses that both the laws of nature and the Word of God were compatible, although it was made clear that God's law counted above all others. According to an ancient Irish legal poem:

'The law of the church is as a sea compared with streams, the law of the church is most wonderful law... It is known that fenechas (inherited common law) is vain in comparison with the words of God, where neither man is defrauded nor God neglected, as a result of which prosperity increases... the law of the church is founded on rocks of truth... it speaks for all conditions of persons...every grade, every kind... It binds, it is not bound; it restrains, it is not restrained; it is appealed to, it does not appeal; it overswears all, it is not oversworn; each one is ignoble compared to it, it is noble compared to all; it is a sea compared with streams.'

The Old Testament was used as a basis for Irish law but it was by no means the sole source. The monks knew that to be effective the law had to relate to people's everyday lives. For instance, Biblical doctrine on the theft of livestock was expanded to include animals that were extremely valuable to ordinary people at the time, namely the horse and the pig. Paganism was of course heresy. But where a seemingly unshakeable belief persisted in pagan gods such as Brigid and Anu, the monks performed the religious equivalent of a corporate takeover by renaming them St Brigid and St Ann and re-launching them as Christian martyrs.

The early church also took careful note of experiences elsewhere in Europe — information which flooded in from the many foreign students who travelled to Ireland in search of learning. The monks, too, set out to discover Britain and the great European powers, further spreading the image of Ireland as the cultural haven of the West. As they roamed they took note of laws tried and tested as fair in other countries. Many ideas were seized upon by the fledgling legislators at home and adapted to Irish circumstances.

Monasteries in 8th and 9th century Ireland had a very different structure to those operating today. They tended to be Christian centres which drew together a number of different churches and churchmen, plus assorted nuns, monks, priests, bishops, virgins and the plain devout. But monasteries also served as political centres for regional kings and a somewhat less holy concoction of soldiers, courtiers, royal favourites, mistresses and, probably, even prostitutes.

The abbots nominally in control of these monastic centres often became extremely rich with massive estates throughout the land. They would live the lives of kings, mixing with society names of the day and patronisng the arts. It was their taste for the trappings of wealth that so encouraged the superb metalwork, artwork and calligraphy that marks Irish culture between the 7th and 10th centuries. In churches the chalices and books shone with ornate gold and silver, the vestments of the priests glittered with minute specks of gold and no self-respecting worshipper would arrive in church without some fancy brooch or bracelet to show off. No wonder the Viking pillagers, once they discovered Ireland's treasures, kept coming back for more.

At this time the Irish Church had two main power bases. The first was Iona, an island off the Scottish coast, where Columba founded a monastery. Iona headed a large group of churches in both Ireland and Scotland and also had influence in Northumbria. Perhaps its greatest leader was the 9th abbot Adomnán (d. 704) who drew up his *Law Of The Innocents*. This was a religious order banning women and children from fighting in wars and protecting women from violent men.

The second great centre was Patrick's church in Armagh; here there was no monastic structure but a succession of bishops who used their links with one of the most powerful families in all Ireland, the Úi Néills, to cement their authority. By the 7th century, so sure was Armagh of its position, that it proclaimed itself the country's principal church and its bishop the primate over all other clergy. What seems clear is that each region had a bishop whose responsibility was for the pastoral care of every type of church in his domain. He would make sure buildings, altars and churchyards were well maintained and he had the power to inflict fines on elders who disobeyed his orders.

This was generally accepted, although it would be wrong to think that the churches had a clear pecking order. There were many different types; those that were 'free' — ie, owned their own lands — and those that were tenants belonging to kings, monasteries or well-off families. There were hundreds of what amounted to parish churches, the humblest of which were no more than crude buildings circled by small graveyards on some nobleman's estate. The local priest would turn up whenever he was available, although there was very often a shortage of clerics whose services were very unreliable.

The church survived, much as it does to this day, by accepting donations from the people. The Irish priests regarded this support as a duty of the laity — part of an unsigned agreement in which the clergy would provide spiritual guidance, conduct birth, marriage and death services, preach God's word, hold mass on Sundays and preside over the major religious festivals. In return worshippers were required to hand over firstlings (the first pick of a crop or harvest) and a tenth of their income, as well as pay for burials. Unsurprisingly, the priests did not always get their dues.

Opposite: *The beautiful Cross of the Scriptures stands in the ruins of Clonmacnoise Monastery, near the River Shannon.*

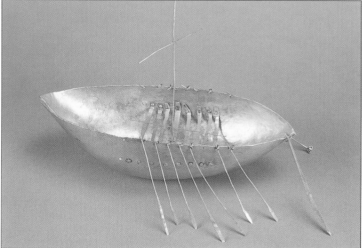

Top: *The Cross of the Scriptures, Clonmacnoise.*

Left: *A golden torc excavated at Clonmacnoise and dating from around the 3rd century BC. Great Christian centres were often founded on earlier, pagan sites.*

Above: *This 1st century AD golden boat, part of the Broighter hoard, had 15 oars, nine seats and a mast with yard arm.*

Opposite: *The Rock of Cashel was the seat of Brian Boru, self-proclaimed king of Ireland. He was crowned in 977.*

Above: *The Irish church was headed in the early years by Iona. Here the cathedral founded by St Columba in AD563 seen from the summit of Dun 1, Iona's highest point, with the Isle of Mull beyond the Sound.*

Left: *Little is known about St Patrick — the patron saint of Ireland, although he was probably not the first missionary. Most stories have Patrick being kidnapped from Britain to Ireland by pirates. From here he escaped to France to study Christianity, and from there he returned in 432 to begin converting the Irish. Here he stands in a grotto at Faha on the Pilgrim's Route up Mount Brandon in Co Kerry.*

Right: *St Patrick's grave in the precincts of the Protestant cathedral at Downpatrick Co Down.*

The Rock of Cashel, the seat of Brian Boru.

GAELIC
FAMILY LIFE

If the Church evolved without rigid structures, the same could not be said of Gaelic society generally. The law was obsessed with a man's status. If you were a peasant seeking compensation for some wrong, your chance of a big payout was infinitely less than if you happened to be the regional king. Because of this, the divisions between the three main classes of kings, lords and commoners were well defined. A king inherited his position, along with lands, power and wealth. A lord was judged not only by his wealth but also by the number of commoners who relied on him for a living. It was sometimes possible for a commoner to claw his way up the social ladder but it was far more usual for hard-up lords — their family assets divided between both legitimate and illegitimate sons down several generations — to end up on the breadline.

Among the commoners there were still more divisions. First among these was the freeman, usually a land-owning farmer who was ensured full legal rights. A typical freeman was described in the 8th century legal document *Crith Gablach* as follows:

'There are always two vessels in his house, a vessel of milk and a vessel of ale. He is a man of three snouts: the snout of a rooting hog which banishes shame at all times, the snout of a bacon pig on the hook, and the snout of plough under the sod, so that he is able to receive king or bishop or scholar or judge from the road, against the arrival of every party of guests. He is a man who has three sacks in his house always for each season: a sack of malt, a sack of sea salt for the salting up of one of his beasts, and a sack of charcoal for iron working, He has seven houses: a corn-kiln, a barn (his share in a mill so that it grinds for him), a dwelling house of 27ft [8.2m], a lean-to of 17ft [5.2m], a pigsty, a calf-fold and a sheep fold. He has 20 cows, two bulls, six oxen, 20 pigs, 20 sheep, four farmyard hogs, two sows, a riding horse with enamelled bridle and 16 sacks of seed corn in the ground. He has a bronze cauldron into which a hog fits. He has parkland in which there are always sheep, without need to change ground. He and his wife have four outfits. His wife is the daughter of his equal, wedded in lawful matrimony.'

Freemen who couldn't quite muster such impressive assets were placed lower in the social scheme of things. Even lower were men with no land or property and below them were the senchleithe, serfs bound to their local lord and master. Most lowly of all were the slaves, freely traded by Gaelic and Viking warlords.

Slaves became especially common between the 9th and 11th centuries and often ended up as subsistence workers in one of the major monasteries. Some slaves were prisoners of war taken by Vikings in foreign lands, others were children snatched with the specific intention of selling them into slavery. In times of famine, poor families would hive off their offspring as slaves as a last resort to prevent starvation.

Above: *The Cashel Folk Park in Co Tipperary provides a fascinating insight into early Gaelic life.*

Opposite: *Round towers such as this at Kells, Co Meath, are often difficult to date. Building methods, designs and techniques were sometimes repeated for hundreds of years.*

The relationship between freemen and lords was called Clientship and was supposed to strike a fair bargain between both. It was in effect a leasing agreement in which the lord would agree to grant his client a 'fief' (usually some livestock or land) and in return the client would make regular payments. There were two categories within the system — free clientship and base clientship.

Free clientship required the freeman to swear himself to the service of his lord, including a promise to fight for him if required. This arrangement allowed noblemen to amass their own private armies which could then be enlisted in the service of a regional king. Free clients were entitled to a share of their master's plunder in any raid or battle but the payment demands on them were high. It was a form of service which lords used to exact heavy rates of interest on the fiefs they advanced.

Base clientship was a rather more work-a-day contract which ensured lords a comfortable standard of living. A lord would first pay the client a handsome advance consistent with his legal standing. Then he would offer him a fief, perhaps of dairy cows, livestock or farm equipment, which would again be tailored to the

man's ability and personal wealth. The lord would also promise to protect him and to fight for him whenever he needed legal compensation for a theft or injury. In return the master could expect a regular supply of food and labour.

The typical annual return on a fief of two dozen dairy cows would be one dairy cow, three calves (of varying quality) half the dripping of a year-old bull, a cauldron of milk, a vessel of cream, 20 loaves, a 10x20cm (4x 8in) pat of butter, two fistfuls of onions, two leeks, and a 0.3m (3ft) long flitch of bacon.

In addition, a lord could invoke a handy clause in the contract entitling him and a group of friends to one night's feasting in the home of the client between each New Year and Shrove Tuesday. For the freeman, this must too often have been a dread occasion. A gluttonous and drunken bunch of nobles would not only eat enough food for two weeks but would quite likely turn a house upside down as well.

Family life was chaotic enough without the input of unwelcome guests such as these. At the lower class levels, two or three families often lived inside a single dwelling. Divorce and re-marriage was widespread, despite the entreaties of the church, and among the nobility it was usual to have a number of wives to ensure a good supply of heirs. This was both a curse and a blessing on the lords. On the one hand they had plenty of reliable manpower available to help manage their estates; but on the other their dynasties were condemned to less and less influence as assets were scattered among generations of heirs.

Ireland in the 7th century had a population of between 500,000 and 1,000,000 people, a level that fluctuated according to the effects of plague or famine. Farming was the driving force of the economy, although huge forests covered much of the countryside and the lowland midlands and western hills were agriculturally poor boglands. With mountains and moorland fringing every kingdom, Ireland was a wilderness punctuated by a scattering of cultural havens (the monasteries) and tens of thousands of small fortified farmsteads.

These farms were built like mini hill-forts with a central roundhouse 6x8m (20-27ft) in diameter surrounded by either an earth rampart (a rath) a dry stone wall (a cashel) or a more-heavily fortified combination of the two (a dun). All farm outbuildings and labourers' quarters were sited inside the enclosure apart from corn kilns (where corn was dried around an oven to circumvent the wet climate) which were thought too much of a fire hazard.

There was also a fourth structure, called a crannog, which was almost certainly imported from Scotland. This was an artificial island in the form of a house-platform at the centre of a shallow lake. It arrived in Ireland quite late — around the 6th century — and was popular because of its obvious defensive qualities. Another British architectural import was probably the souterrain, found only in Ulster. This was a stone-built, oddly-shaped underground chamber; history has shed no light on its purpose.

There was no straw on Irish farms, land was instead kept in reserve for winter grazing, and only the rich had a mill (or even a share in one). Cultivated land was divided into strips near the farmyard while livestock would be sent out in summer to graze common ground on the moors. Responsibility for tending these animals would fall on to the women, as would the salting of butter and cheese making — both vital for building up winter food supplies. Milk formed a major part of the diet, cow's milk for the rich, sheep's milk for the poor.

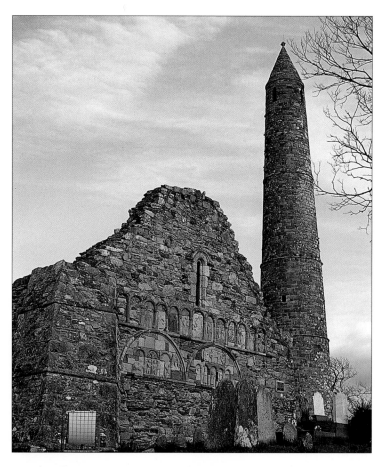

Above: *More round towers at Ardmore, Co Waterford, Clonmacnoise Monastery* **Opposite left** *and Timahoe, Co Laois,* **Opposite right**. *The towers had obvious defensive qualities in a land where Gaelic chiefs were perpetually at war with each other.*

Ploughing would begin in March. A sure sign of a farmer's wealth was ownership of a full plough and oxen team; lowlier families had to make do with spades. The most important crops were oats (used for porridge and crude bread), barley (for beer and bread), wheat (used to make bread for sale to the very wealthy) and corn. Vegetable production was small scale and apples were just about the only cultivated fruit, although families used wild berries and nuts to supplement their diet.

This was not an economy in which food was widely traded. Families worked to keep themselves alive and a failure of the crops, or widespread disease in livestock, had catastrophic results. Famine increased the likelihood of death from diseases such as smallpox, dysentery, pneumonia and rabies. Disease resulted in whole communities shifting around (which spread more disease) and in the worst years civil unrest erupted.

The most convenient authority to blame for disaster was the church, which responded in the only way it could by sending high-profile emissaries out to the worst affected areas with relics of the saints and prayers for deliverance. At these times the doctrines of Christianity would be openly challenged by many who still held a candle for the old magic and the pagan gods. The bishops relied heavily on the passing of new laws demanding respect for God and curbing violence among the masses. Without the practical support of the regional kings and their armies the Church's task would have been nigh on impossible.

THE VIKING WARS

The wind is fierce tonight
It tosses the sea's white hair
I fear no wild Vikings
Sailing the quiet main

Thus wrote a 9th century Irish monk along the margin of his manuscript as he sat shivering in a cheerless cell. His simple prose perfectly sums up the mood of the time; an era when no coastal settlement was safe and every church and monastery lived in fear of the plundering longboat crews.

Ireland, like the rest of Europe, was living the nightmare of defending against these strong, fearless warriors capable of mounting lightening-fast attacks with ruthless efficiency. The Vikings came for plunder, for political expediency, for colonial ambition and for new commercial opportunities. To the Irish kings, for whom centuries of continuous strife had always involved the same standard military scenario, the effect must have been shattering.

The Vikings earliest known assault on Ireland came in 795AD when they burned Rathlin. Over the following four decades there was sporadic raiding of the coast, these appear to be mainly treasure-hunting escapades. In 798 the St Patrick's Island monastery near Skerries, Co Dublin was burned and the shrine of the monastery's patron, Dochonna, broken up. The Norsemen also demanded a heavy tax or tribute on the surrounding farming community. This was payable in heads of cattle — a heavy blow to the fragile rural economy.

Mostly the invading crews were Norwegian, called Finn-gaill (White Foreigners) but there were also a few Danes Dubb-gaill (Black Foreigners). Quite how and why the Irish writers of the day used these colours to distinguish between their foes is a mystery. To most people the invaders were simply Norsemen — men who would publicly hang three-score of their prisoners at once; who would gleefully sack and burn whole towns, and who would snatch loved-ones at will for sale into slavery.

The Vikings though didn't have it all their own way. Historians of the day recorded how in 811 Ulaid warriors wiped out a band of raiders, how the following year another group was slaughtered by the Co Mayo-based Umall and how the king of the Eoganacht, Locha Léin, inflicted devastation on a coastal war party. Yet these were small victories — in the eye of the gathering Viking storm, they were of no significance.

In the 830s the Norwegian attacks became much larger military operations. The first push inland came in 836 when Vikings poured into the territories of the southern Úi Néill, seized hundreds of captives and killed many more. Within 12 months Norse fleets of up to 60 ships were sailing into the rivers Boyne and Liffey in what was surely a terrifying spectacle for the locals. With their garish red, gold and green sails, bows ornately carved with evil-looking monsters and the sun flashing off shields lashed to their sides, such fleets must have seemed like the Devil's own navy coming to visit.

It is worth mentioning here the design of the longboats because it was this design, as much as the ferocity of the soldiers on board, that gave the Vikings such an edge. A boat of the Gokstad type, typical of the 9th century, would be around 22m (75ft) long, 5.5m (18ft) in the beam and with a keel of almost 17.5m (58ft) hewn from a single piece of oak. The hull would be supported by some 19 frames and cross beams and was overlaid with a pine deck (some planks often left loose to permit storage below the waterline). Each carried around 32 crewmen — these were not ships made to move large armies — and relied mostly on sail power.

With a favourable wind and sea, the Gokstad vessel was easily capable of voyaging 120 miles a day, allowing on-board supplies to be kept to a minimum. But the ship's greatest attribute was its ability to manoeuvre superbly close to shore. A draft of around 1m (3ft) allowed it to discharge warriors directly onto a beach, and often the Irish would know nothing of an attack until the moment it happened. On the very few occasions they tried to pursue the invaders, their task was hopeless. The Vikings would simply turn into the wind and make off by oar, leaving their victims' cumbersome ships floundering behind.

The first Viking to leave a permanent mark on Ireland was Turgeis, from Norway, who arrived in 840 with a powerful fleet on the north coast. He quickly established himself as the head of all Norsemen in Erin and soon had most of Ulster under his control. His capture of Armagh brought him fabulous wealth and immense power and he and his kin are credited with establishing the great Viking settlements of Dublin, Wexford, Waterford, Cork and Limerick. He is said to have robbed the monasteries of Clonmacnois and Clonfert and encouraged scores of renegade Christians to troop into churches to transform them into heathen temples. In Armagh he was said to have settled himself down at the altar declaring that he was the heathen High-priest. At the altar of Clonmacnois his wife Ota reportedly chanted spells to Thor. How much of this was true, and how much the fevered imaginings of outraged monks, is difficult to tell. But it is possible that Turgeis tried to package himself as a leader by promoting sacrifice as a way of ensuring favourable seasons.

Opposite: *Carlingford — home of the Danish Viking fleet in 850BC. Two years later Carlingford Lough was the scene of a major naval engagement between Danes and Norwegians.*

Throughout the 840s Viking aggression reached a new peak of intensity and for the first time a fleet appeared on Lough Neagh. The crews first systematically robbed the monasteries and villages around its shores and then pushed out in search of greater booty — first to Louth (where they captured leading churchmen and scholars), then to Armagh, and finally to Dublin, from where they harried Leinster in 842. Their Dublin settlement included a warriors' cemetery at Kilmainham, to the west of the city, from which archaeologists have since recovered a number of important finds.

For a time it seemed as though Ireland would be swamped by the invaders. The Shannon river system was in Viking control, great cultural centres such as Clonmacnoise, Seir, Birr and Clonfert were sacked and a steady flow of riches from the nation's monasteries were transported to the Norsemen's formidable garrisons at Dublin, Waterford, Youghal, Wexford, St Mullins, Cork and on the Shannon estuary. Yet already the new settlers were doing deals with the natives — one alliance between Viking and Irish in 842 resulted in the death of the abbot of Linn Duachail.

But Turgeis and his like were not unbeatable. Away from the coast — where Viking naval power was unmatched — they were just local kings as vulnerable as any other. So it transpired in 845 when Turgeis was captured by Mael Seachlainn, king of Meath, and drowned in Lough Owel. That same year the abbot of Terryglass and Clonenagh and the deputy abbot of Kildare took up arms against the invaders — among several leading churchmen to do so. Both were killed in action at Dunamase.

Turgeis's death heralded a bad run for the Norwegian Vikings and they suffered a series of reverses. Ironically, the worst of these was inflicted not by the Irish but by a strong force of Danes which in 850 put into Carlingford Lough in Co Down and set up a garrison. The following year they pushed into Dublin where they routed the Norwegians and rewarded their Irish allies with much silver and gold. But Danish control of Dublin was short-lived. In 853 a large contingent of Norwegian royal ships under Prince Olaf Amlaibh arrived in Ireland and most Danes and Norwegians quickly accepted him as undisputed Norse leader. Some Danes fled to England, unable to live as inferiors, while a few Irish kings were forced to pay heavy *wergeld* (compensation) for the death of Turgeis.

Olaf ruled much of southern Ireland for the next 18 years, his sovereignty occasionally disrupted by voyages back to his homeland (for reasons unclear). His brother Ivar, Lord of Limerick, minded the shop while he was away but the nation was still far from being dominated. The more powerful Irish kings were in no mood to cower and in 866 Finnliath, king of the northern Úi Néill, went on the rampage along the north coast destroying many Viking garrisons. By now, apart from a few irregular attacks, the first wave of the Norse invasion was over. Olaf died in Norway in 871 and Ivar and his heirs proved unable to rule with the same authority. Over the next few decades the Irish kings once more began to extend their influence.

But the Norsemen had not forgotten Ireland and in the early 10th century they returned in force. A large fleet sailed into Waterford harbour in 914 and this was reinforced by further ships the following year. The plundering began all over again — especially in Munster and Leinster — and when the high king of the Úi Néills , Niall Glúndub, tried to drive them out he failed to achieve an overall victory. First his Leinster army was routed and then he and his greatest warriors were killed in the Battle of Dublin (919). Over the next 30 or so years the Vikings reigned unchallenged,

although they became more and more preoccupied with strengthening their hold across the water in York. From 950 onwards there were few new raids and the Norsemen's influence was now as settlers and traders, rather than invaders.

Arguments still rage about the ways the Vikings changed early Ireland. They certainly brought a revolution in the importance of navies as military forces and their trading brought untold riches into the country — itself a boost to the economy. On the negative side they butchered and executed many of their opponents (often unnecessarily), destroyed scores of sacred sites and stole many Celtic treasures. Yet the level of violence they employed was hardly new. The Irish kings were every bit as bloodthirsty and equally capable of robbing a monastery or two when they had the mind. From an abbot's point of view it made little difference whether an attacker was a murderous Viking or a murderous Irishman — the toll in lives and treasure was pretty much the same.

In fact, despite all the depredations, most of the Irish monasteries survived intact. This is partly because the Irish Vikings tended to concentrate their forces in specific, defendable areas rather than trying to hold down entire kingdoms as they did in England. There was certainly no Irish equivalent of the Danelaw, the huge tract of Viking-controlled country north of a line between Chester and the Thames. So it was business as usual for the Irish monks; at Cork, for instance, they lived side by side with the Norsemen, only occasionally enduring a raid. Such was their tenacity that there was never once a break in the succession of abbots.

Some have tried to suggest that the Vikings 'heathenised' Ireland by encouraging married clergy, lay abbots and nepotism in church and government offices. However all these vices existed before anyone had heard of the Norsemen and remained long after they had been absorbed into the genetic stock. Keeping a sought-after church position within the family was accepted behaviour in the 7th century, and common in the 8th. Later, it may have been convenient for the Church to blame the invaders. In fact, after a few generations, there was increasingly little to tell the Vikings and the native Gaelic kings apart.

Above: *When they weren't fighting, Vikings enjoyed a mental challenge. This game board dates from around the ninth century.*

Opposite above: *A hand carved model long boat.*

Opposite below: *A well-preserved Viking coin.*

KINGS AT WAR

Whatever their habitual excesses, Gaelic kings were regarded as useful allies by the Church. They were able to impose order, by force if necessary. They could carry out capital punishments (something the early Irish bishops were all in favour of) and they were a powerful ally in ensuring God's law was followed. It was for this reason that the bishops courted royal patronage by consecrating kings, a practice later adopted elsewhere in Europe.

Kings were to be revered and respected and they were entitled to their taxes (though of course not from the church). But the bishops also encouraged fair and civilised behaviour among rulers. They were not to mount raids against their own people or impose punitive taxes; neither could they pass unjust laws.

Surprising as it may seem, the Church held great influence over the kingships and its authority was rarely challenged. When in 809 the Ulaid tribe attacked a church belonging to Armagh, and killed its priest-in-charge, the powerful King Áed Oirnide exacted terrible revenge by invading their lands and putting Ulaid leaders to the sword.

But who were these kings and how did they carve up the country? This remains one of the most confusing features of early Christian Ireland, not least because historians of the day tended to over-egg the pudding in recording the great adventures and victories of their rulers. Occasionally, claims would be made of the emergence of a *tríath* a single High King said to rule 'through the kingdoms of Ireland from sea to sea.' This implies that his subjects were aware of — and accepted — an all-conquering lord and master. In fact there is little evidence to back this and if a tríath did surface his tenure must have been brief. Ireland, with its ever-expanding genetic melting pot of native Irish, Briton, Celt, Roman, Gaul and Scandinavian, was anything but a united kingdom.

Nonetheless, many leading scholars of the time were keen to promote the myth of togetherness. By the 7th century much frenzied research was going on into ancestry and the *Book of the Taking of Ireland* later argued that all the great families and dynasties were actually united by descent from a single group of ancestors. This idea became a shibboleth which proved hard to dismantle, even though it was fiction. It was a convenient way for some warring kings to wrap their petty feuding in the cloak of unity.

The class system applied to kings as much as it did to commoners. There were the *rí túaithe* ('petty kings' with limited lands), the *ruiri* (supposedly overlords of several rí túaithe) and the *rí ruirech*, or provincial kings. For many years it was the petty kings who held sway and their kingdoms expanded or contracted according to the bargains they struck and the alliances they made. But by the 8th century they were really no more than landed noblemen. Real power lay in the hands of the family dynasties who ruled and contested the provinces. Of these dynasties the greatest was the Úi Néill, although even they were sub-divided into branches and feuding factions. No one should blame students of the period for feeling bewildered by it all.

The Úi Néills claimed to be Kings of Tara, a phrase traditionally taken to mean high kings of all-Ireland. Their ancestor was a warrior called Niall Noígiallach, one of the barbarian Irish who raided the western shores of Britain during the Roman occupation and who even ventured as far as the Isle of Wight. His ancient seat was *Ràth na Ríogh* (Fort of the Kings) at Tara, Co Meath, which some believe was the centre of a fifth Irish province, called Mide. The 'Stone of Destiny', a stone structure within the fort, was said to have been the place where kings were crowned, although the stone was originally a phallic symbol used in the fertility rights of a much earlier culture. Whatever secrets it holds, Tara was certainly a settlement of major historical significance. Roman objects dating to the 3rd century AD have been found on the site, suggesting that travellers or Roman soldiers on campaign were received there.

The Úi Néill ruled much of Ulster, the north-west and the midlands. There is some doubt about when the family split into its two main branches — the northern and southern Úi Néill — nor is it clear precisely why the split occurred. The politics is further complicated by the separation of the southern group into two factions (the Síl nAeda Sláine and the Clann Cholmáin) and the northern group into two more (Cenél Conaill and Cenél nEógain). From time to time rulers would claim over-kingship of the entire Úi Néill clan. The first of these rose from the Clann Cholmáin in 743 and, with one exception, this faction kept its stranglehold on the overkingship for more than a century. But power in Ireland has never been a certainty. For hundreds of years the Úi Neills squabbled amongst themselves and with the powerful tribes from the south. It was only when the Vikings arrived in force that the Irish began to appear more unified. Even then, it was a unity born of necessity rather than desire.

Elsewhere in Ireland the feuding was much the same. In the 8th century the Úi Dúnlainge ruled much of Leinster, allying themselves closely with the bishops of Kildare and fighting regularly with their rivals, the Úi Chennselaig, in the south. Leinster gradually fell under Úi Néill influence and by the mid-9th century its kings had installed puppet rulers to govern on their behalf.

Connacht's two mighty dynasties were the Úi Fiachrach and the Úi Briúin (both claimed ancestral links with the Úi Néill). For

Opposite: *A statue portraying the death of Ireland's greatest mythological hero, Cu Chulainn, stands in the General Post Office, O'Connell Street, Dublin. The adventures of Cu Chulainn are recounted in the epic Gaelic prose of* The Tain.

much of the 7th century the province was controlled by Úi Fiachrach but once the Úi Briúin emerged it gained ground fast. By 725 it had established an aggressive nobility and regional government which provided a base from which to seek power over the entire country.

In Munster the Eóganacht dominated between the 7th and mid-10th centuries. It had a proud history on the battlefield and its King Cathal (721-42) was hailed King of Ireland (mainly by his Munster subjects). The Eóganacht's claim to produce the country's most Christian kings was, however, dealt a severe knock by the actions of King Feidlimid, who died in 847. He was ordained Bishop of Munster but devoted much of his time to sacking monasteries such as Kildare, Durrow, Fore and Gallen. He was an accomplished general and his raids on the Úi Néill forced them to meet him for peace talks. Yet by the mid-900s the peace had crumbled and the Eoganacht quickly became a spent force. Its place was taken by the Dál Cais of north Munster.

The story of the Dál Cais, and its titanic struggle against the Úi Néill, is a key period in Irish history. It is the story of how Ireland almost achieved its Holy Grail, the crowning of an undisputed high king. Almost... but not quite.

In 976 Brian Boru became king of Dál Cais and within three years both Limerick and Munster were totally under his control. He struck a deal with the Ostmen (the name the Vikings now called themselves) of Waterford to use their fleet and then marched on into Connacht and Leinster. He was engaged by Mael Sechnaill II, the overking of the Úi Néill, but there was no decisive battle and in 997 the two rulers sat down at Clonfert to carve up Ireland between them. Brian got Dublin and Leinster to add to his kingdom but it was not enough to satisfy him. After crushing an uprising in Dublin he set out on a mission to conquer the entire country and by 1011 he seemed on the verge of success. The Úi Néill was in tatters and no other provincial king could muster a realistic force against him. Then came news of another revolt in Dublin and Leinster.

The revolt was orchestrated by Dublin Ostmen and backed by their Viking friends from the Isle of Man and the Western Isles. They marched against Brian and fought one of the bloodiest battles in Irish history at Clontarf during Easter 1014. Brian's army won, although he died in battle on Good Friday, along with many capable leaders on both sides. Trying to work out what actually happened at Clontarf is a tricky business. If any records of the battle were made then they were eagerly passed on to the saga writers — the authors of the heroic tales which blend fact with folklore in Norse and Celtic tradition. As a result, the battle was depicted as a great struggle between the Irish and the Vikings for control of the nation — this was not so. The Vikings were by now well settled and scattered and certainly not an occupying army. The battle of Clontarf was far more about the ambitions and petty rivalries of Irish leaders. Its sad legacy was that it ended the life of the one man who really could have united the provinces of Ireland under one throne — Brian Boru.

According to the sagas, the two sides faced each other between Tolka and Liffey, a few kilometers inland from Dublin Bay. Those fighting for Brian and 'Ireland' included Brian's son Murchad, his grandson Tordelbach, Mael Seachlainn and his warriors from the southern Úi Néill and Ospak, of the Isle of Man. Against them, their flanks partly guarded by the sea, were the 'Vikings' — Sigurd the Stout of Orkney, Brodir of Man, Maelmordha with his Leinster army and the Dublin ostmen under Dubhgall. This was a battle in which Viking fought against Viking and Irishman against Irishman. Even brothers ended up on different sides.

The saga writers didn't let them down. There were stories of how Brian Boru's ex-wife Gormflaith was promised as a prize of victory (along with Dublin as a dowry) to both Sigurd and Brodir. How the Icelander Hall of Sida coolly knelt to tie his bootlace as his men fled from the advancing Irish. Asked why he had not run he replied: 'I cannot get home tonight, for my home is out in Iceland.' His life was spared. Then there was the death of Brian himself, slaughtered as he knelt praying for God's help in Tomar's Wood. Brian's son Murchad was killed within an ace of victory and the grandson Tordelbach drowned as he hunted enemy soldiers near the weir of Clontarf. In all 4,000 of Brian's men, and 7,000 of their opponents (including the leaders Sigurd and Brodir) fell in battle — many of them fell as they fled back to their Dublin stronghold and their ships.

The Úi Néill high king Mael Sechnaill II hoped to fill Brian's shoes but in reality he was just another provincial ruler with big ambitions. For a century and a half Ireland returned to a familiar political minefield with only Turlough O'Connor, king of Connacht, emerging as a contender for true national power. When he died, the leading force was once again an Úi Néill — this time Muirchertach Mac Lochlainn.

Mac Lochlainn allied himself with the king of Leinster, Dermot MacMurrough, and together they decided to wrest control of Dublin. The city — still dominated by Viking noblemen despite the result at Clontarf — was by now undisputed capital of the nation. Far from being kicked out, the Vikings had continued trading, maintained their kings and princes and replenished their treasure chests. Dublin was among the greatest cities of the Viking world, an economic goldmine and a place where ambitious rulers could hire high quality, Norse-trained mercenaries. He who ruled it, could rule Ireland.

But the Dubliners had some powerful allies in the form of Rory O'Connor, king of Connacht, and the one-eyed king of Bréifne, Tighearnán O'Rourke. Together this alliance fought successfully against Mac Lochlainn, who died in battle in 1166. An isolated Dermot MacMurrough was driven out and found himself devoid of any powerbase. O'Rourke, whose wife Dervorgilla had been abducted by Dermot 14 years earlier, exacted revenge by insisting that his sworn enemy was removed from the Leinster throne.

Dermot decided he must regain his rightful seat by force and he fled to England to enlist a mercenary force. In doing so he changed the course of Irish history. By inviting the English to help him he sparked the Norman invasion of Ireland and destroyed forever the dream of a native Irish High King.

Opposite: *Early art decorates a grave at Newgrange, the legendary seat and burial place of Ireland's greatest Gaelic kings. For centuries the mound at Newgrange was believed to conceal an entrance to the land of the pagan gods.*

THE NORMAN INVASION

The victory of Rory O'Connor over Dermot MacMurrough and Muirchertach Mac Lochlainn resulted in Rory crowning himself high king of Ireland in 1166 (a purely theoretical claim). Dermot swore to take revenge and the same year he travelled to England to ask the young King Henry II for help in raising an army. But Henry was cautious. His power in England was still shaky and he saw little profit in getting dragged in to a conflict far out to the west. Instead he granted his Norman barons permission to aid Dermot, if they so wished.

Dermot began his recruitment drive in Bristol, a port which had long had close contacts with Dublin. He signed up three of the most powerful Welsh lords — Richard Fitz Gilbert de Clare and the half-brothers Maurice FitzGerald and Robert FitzStephen, sons of the Welsh princess Nesta. Dermot promised de Clare (nicknamed Strongbow) the hand of his daughter Aoife and the whole of Leinster. FitzGerald and FitzStephen were offered Wexford and surrounding lands.

It proved an effective alliance. Between 1169 and 1171 the Normans retook Leinster, including Dublin, and began expanding outwards into Meath and Bréifne. Henry realised their ambitions were far greater than he had imagined and belatedly tried to stall them by ordering a ban on exports to Ireland, with the intention of cutting off their supply line. He also instructed Strongbow not to enter Ireland — an unreasonable and unrealistic demand seeing as the baron was already there!

By the late summer of 1171, Henry realised he could dally no longer. Dermot MacMurrough had died in May and Strongbow had enforced the deal making himself new Lord of Leinster. Attempts by the Leinstermen to revolt had been ruthlessly crushed and Henry now faced the prospect of a new, independent Norman kingdom on his vulnerable western seaboard. On 17 October 1171 the king landed near Waterford in command of a large, well-trained army and prepared to stamp his authority on the situation.

It was perhaps the first time in 400 years that an invading force arrived without any kind of fight. Strongbow had intercepted the king before Henry had even left England, begged forgiveness and promised that Leinster would be held only as a fief. Perhaps in awe of Henry's power, the Irish kings quickly followed suit. On the leisurely march to Dublin they lined up to pay homage — the chiefs of Leinster, Cork's King Dermot MacCarthy, Limerick's Donal Mór O'Brien, Bréifne's Tighearnán O'Rourke, Airgialla's Murchadh O'Carroll and the king of the Ulaid, Donn Slébhe MacDunleavy.

Nationalists with a romantic view of Ireland later agonised over such dismal resistance to the invading 'English'. But, as historians have pointed out, Irish kings had little to lose and, perhaps, the chance of protecting their own lands and interests from accession. In any case, none of them had much notion of unity and mistrusted each other every bit as much as they mistrusted Henry.

Henry presented himself as a reformer of the Irish Church, but he had to tread carefully. The English Archbishop St Thomas Becket — murdered by Henry's hit men for trying to assert church independence — was not long dead and it was too soon for the king to proclaim his papal authority over Ireland. He began by convening a great synod, or national gathering, of Irish church leaders in the winter of 1171/2. The aim was to organise the Irish clergy on similar lines to the English system and, allegedly, to improve discipline and moral fibre.

Far from opposing Henry, the Irish bishops, like the kings, welcomed him. After Henry's penance and reconciliation with the Church in May 1172, they sent a steady stream of letters to Pope Alexander III extolling the great improvements he had made. Predictably, the Pope confirmed Henry's right to rule Ireland, urged him to defend the Church, warned the Irish kings to stick by their oaths of allegiance and instructed the bishops to excommunicate any who disobeyed.

Left: *The Norman barbican at St Lawrence's Gate, Drogheda, Co Louth, dominated the castle's walled defences. The first fortifications in the town were probably constructed by Hugh de Lacy in the 1180s.*

Opposite: *A sundial stands in the grounds of Kilmalkeadar Church on Co Kerry's Dingle Peninsula.*

Henry left Wexford on 17 April, 1172, his attention drawn elsewhere in his kingdom. Behind him he left garrisons in Dublin and other major seaports (such as Cork and Limerick) and granted his own Norman favourites land and income rights in Dublin. One of his loyalist supporters, Hugh de Lacy, was given Meath and later became constable of Dublin. He effectively acted as governor of Ireland and wasted no time killing Tighearnán O'Rourke (in the middle of a so-called parley). By 1175 he and Strongbow had quelled the last few pockets of Irish resistance and set about dividing the country up into baronies to be distributed among their own friends and supporters.

That same year, 1175, Rory O'Connor signed the Treaty of Windsor with Henry, which named Rory as high-king of all Ireland outside Leinster, Meath and Waterford. Rory had most to lose from Henry's arrival because he still saw himself as Ireland's overall ruler. The Treaty of Windsor was billed as a great coup for him but, like so many other Crown deals, it withered on the vine. Rory was soon told he could have Connacht alone — and then only if he paid the tributes demanded.

Neither Henry nor Rory were able to control their followers properly. The invading Norman barons grabbed land where they could, taking little notice of Crown instructions, while the Limerick king Donal Mór O'Brien burnt the town to prevent it becoming a Norman garrison. But though he had not planned colonisation, Henry began to have more of a stake in making it work. In 1177 he made his son, Prince John, Lord of Ireland and went back on promises to keep the kingdoms of Meath, Limerick and Cork for their respective Irish leaders. Soon the country was being governed by Dublin-based bureaucrats who according to King Henry's own advisor, Gerald of Wales, were 'neither loyal to their subjects nor formidable to their enemies.'

The Norman rush to colonise Ireland was fuelled by a sharp rise in the population of Europe. Food prices were high; labour costs were low and there was a steady migration of people in search of better living conditions. The sparsely populated Irish countryside with its rich farming potential was therefore an economic magnet to the power-hungry barons. They received feudal grants to defend their new territories and this resulted in boom time for builders of motte and bailey castles. The motte was a high, circular earthen mound within which rose the bailey, a strong wooden (or occasionally stone) tower. Once these baronies were well established the Normans looked to create towns nearby, places where they could trade the food surplus produced by their labourers. Kilkenny, Trim and New Ross all evolved in this way, attracting much foreign immigration.

According to a poll of Dublin's merchants at the end of the 13th century the new citizens were arriving from throughout England and Wales, as well as from France and Flanders. These people were not only knights and noblemen, many hundreds of colonists were peasants and cottiers who, despite a lowly birth, were made freemen in the new land. To make way for them, the native Irish were pushed out from the best farmland to the barren forests, mountains and marshlands.

Only one Irish family made it into the ranks of the Norman nobility — the FitzDermots of Rathdown, whose ancestors were sometime supporters of Strongbow. The rest lived almost as exiles in their own land, often in small, isolated communities, although they still had to pay their taxes and they could be requisitioned to fight on behalf of their lords. For many of these serfs or *betaghs* life was not much changed. For others, such as the poorer landowners,

the Normans' arrival meant demotion. No longer were they classed as free. As betaghs they were bound to the soil and the service of their lord.

In the eastern plains the Normans imposed their language and culture quickly. Norman-French became the language of the aristocracy and, in Dublin, the wattle architecture of the Vikings was replaced by large, timber-framed houses and an ever-expanding use of stonework. Among the great churches, which until now had been constructed in Irish-Romanesque style, there appeared a new trend imported from Britain — the Early English Gothic style. The raw materials for these buildings came from England, as did the decorative stone carvings and gargoyles.

Even greater changes began to appear in the Irish economic structure. Viking trade aside, Ireland had been largely a subsistence economy. Now that the Norman lords were running more efficient farms, the country was transformed into a wealth-generating market economy. Seaports along the eastern coast flourished on the trade in surplus fruit, crops and vegetables to England and the continent. This income enabled the barons to build their great stone fortresses of the 13th century, symbols of their power, their wealth and their system of justice.

As the lord of Ireland (later king of England as well) Prince John was suspicious of everyone, even his father's Dublin governor Hugh de Lacy. At first he treated the Irish chiefs with disdain and contempt, although after becoming king he realised the need for more diplomatic language to retain their loyalty. Under John the system of government became a monstrous bureaucracy in which his King's Council seemed to breed civil servants. As the 13th century progressed, these men met regularly with the principal Norman barons. The Great Councils, as they were called, became the basis for an Irish Parliament.

Yet even now, the seeds of Irish nationalism were being sown. The bards composed prophecies detailing some of the terrible things which would one day happen to the Normans (these were really adaptations of similar sentiments voiced against the Vikings) and there was talk of a messenger from God. In 1214 there was much excitement when a holy man calling himself Aodh the Deliverer emerged claiming he was the fulfilment of a prophecy. He was later found to be a fraud.

In their songs and poems, the folksingers began to foster a hatred for their new colonial masters. One poem of the period, written in the kingdom of Bréifne, swears revenge for the Norman murder of King Tighearnán O'Rourke:

Opposite: *A typical Norman gate set into the walls at Wexford. Efficient defences constructed by the invaders forced native Gaelic chiefs to re-assess their battlefield tactics. No longer could they dictate the rules of engagement.*

Numerous will be their powerful wiles
Their fetters and their manacles
Numerous their lies and executions
And their secure stone houses...

Though great you deem the success of the Foreigners
You noble men of Ireland
The glorious Angel tells me
That the Bréifnians will avenge Tighearnàn

Poems such as these became the forerunners of the first Irish protest songs. Many hundreds of years later, similar sentiments would emerge from the Irish nationalists fighting for self-rule.

Below: *One of several round towers which controlled the city walls of Waterford. The fortifications probably date from the mid-13th century.*

Opposite: *A Romanesque doorway at Kilmore, Co Cavan.*

Overleaf: *The small, though well-designed, castle at Claregalway, Co Galway is based on Norman ideas and dates from around the 16th century. Its defensive features include a 'murder hole' — an opening from which the castle's occupants could direct fire onto unsuspecting assailants.*

HILLFORTS
AND CASTLES

There are somewhere around 50 hillforts across Ireland, mostly scattered in the south of the country. They are thought to have been built during the Iron Age, or possibly Late Bronze Age, but their exact purpose remains a matter of debate. Some were sited at such a high altitude — Caherconree, Co Kerry, for example lies at 610m (1,800ft) — as to make full-time occupation unlikely. Is it possible the forts offered temporary refuge to which tribes retreated in times of unrest? Were they centres of government? Or were they primitive stadia for annual festivals and gatherings? All we can say with certainty is that they seem to fall into three main categories.

The first type are forts with just a single rampart, often surrounding a defensible hilltop or burial mound. Some historians have argued that Iron Age builders deliberately picked cairns and sacred sites to give their construction an aura of respectability — a bridging of old and new cultures. This is a neat theory, but it doesn't always fit the evidence. At Freestone Hill Fort, Co Kilkenny, the builders don't appear to have given a fig for the sanctity of the graves of their ancestors; to save hauling too much stone from outside the immediate area they simply demolished the Bronze Age cairns around them.

The second category of hillfort, more common in the southwest, has two or more well-spaced earth ramparts and occasionally features stone walls as additional defences. There are a number of excellent examples — Ballylin, Co Limerick (which covers 202sq m [50 acres] and is among the biggest), Mooghaun North, Co Clare, the Grianán of Aileach, Co Donegal, and the spectacular Dún Aenghus, on the Aran Isles. Dún Aenghus also makes use of a defensive measure known as chevaux-de-frise, in which massive blocks of stone are placed in an irregular jumble to slow down advancing warriors. Some historians have suggested this technique was brought to Ireland by Spanish or Portuguese settlers fleeing the Roman conquest of Europe. The idea is certainly possible, though unproven.

The third category covers three promontory forts — Luriegethan and Knockdhu, in Co Antrim, and Caherconree (mentioned above). The Antrim sites may have been constructed by invaders voyaging up the Irish Sea from Britain or France.

It is impossible to know how long hillforts remained in active use. However the centuries between the arrival of Christianity in Ireland, and the Viking Wars, may have seen them occupied temporarily as strategically important ground during tribal wars. By the time the Normans arrived in Ireland only seven fortresses of significance were mentioned — and these were more likely to have been timber constructions.

Castle building got into full swing following the Norman invasion and continued right up until the Cromwellian campaign of the mid-i17th century. As building work could be carried out only during periods of relative peace and stability, the first Norman castles were rather thrown together. They comprised a motte — a mound of earth dug out from a circular ditch — on which a wooden tower would be constructed as the baron's personal residence. To one side of the motte would be the bailey, a flat enclosed area encompassing a hall, chapel, kitchen, stables, barns and smithy.

In Ireland these castles are of vastly differing size and shape. Some were considered useful enough to be habitable as late as the 15th century, while others were little more than observation posts and were quickly abandoned once Norman control became well established. Almost all the motte and bailey castles date from before 1216, though other than that little is known of their history. So many records were destroyed in Ireland's traumatic past that almost every medieval building has to be dated by comparing it to similar structures in Britain.

The country's oldest mortared stone castles are probably at Carrickfergus, Dundrum and Carlingford — all these date from between 1185-1200. Other early examples are Dublin, Kilkenny and Limerick, each constructed between 1205 and 1230 and each featuring a quadrangular court with high corner towers and a double-tower gatehouse. Later, rectangular courts with D-shaped towers came into vogue as at Roscommon Castle; built by Edward I on similar lines to his massive fortress at Harlech in North Wales.

Conditions inside these early castles were rudimentary and far from private. Glass windows were virtually unknown (wooden shutters were used instead) and to make the most of the available light, the walls were painted with whitewash. Some of the more important rooms had rugs or wicker mats and occasionally biblical paintings and tapestries. Latrines were built into the castle walls — the resulting smell from below can only be imagined — but there was little privacy for anyone. Even the lord and his wife would share their bedroom with several senior servants, relying only on a curtain around their bed to keep out prying eyes. Lowlier household members would have to make rough beds out of rushes and lie around the fire in the main hall, or perhaps in the kitchen. If a bed was available, four or five people at a time would have to huddle together inside it to keep warm.

Furniture was a rare luxury and usually of simple design. A lord and lady would usually have their own personal chairs in a hall or bedchamber; the rest of the servants would have to make do with benches. Apart from this, the only other furniture would be a few large tables and wooden chests for storing clothes, plate, cooking utensils and family heirlooms.

Opposite: *Reflections of the past — the ruins of Dromineer Castle, Co Tipperary.*

By the days of the Cromwellian campaign, living conditions were better and furnishings rather more elaborate. A report prepared by Hardress Waller, owner of Castletown Tower, Co Limerick, on valubles captured from him by Irish rebels gives some idea of what the landed classes of the time regarded as valuable. Waller lists:

'Eleven downe and feather beds, six flocke beds with boulsters, pillowes, blancketts, rugs and caddoes (rough overblankets) to the said beds. Candlesticks, chamberpotts, stills (distilleries) and such like things of pewter and brasse. Hangings for a large dyning room and two chambers of tapestrie and divers other hangings and curtaynes for windows. Two very rich Turkey carpetts. A clocke. A chest of books.'

The period between 1310 and 1430 saw little new castle building in Ireland. The invasion of Edward Bruce, the general economic decline in Europe and the ravages of the Black Death meant few barons had either the time or the money to devote to extra defences. The Gaelic chieftains, who were therefore enjoying something of a comeback, built a few plain towers (probably Buncrana, Co Donegal and Roslee, Co Sligo were among these) but they were far too busy destroying abandoned Norman fortresses to bother about building their own. One notable exception is the Archbishop of Dublin's castle at Swords, Co Dublin, which appears to be 14th century.

In 1429 the Irish Parliament approved a £10 subsidy to landowners in the English Pale counties of Dublin, Meath, Kildare and Louth to improve defences. This sparked off a spate of tower building, mostly to the modest specifications required by the statute — towers had to be a minimum of 15m (40ft) high, 6m (20ft) long and 5m (16ft) wide. They incorporated a number of designs peculiar to Ireland, such as parapet machicolations (slots for shooting arrows or dropping stones) above the entrances, double-stepped battlements and murder holes (openings set in the roof of an entranceway down which stones could be dropped). There are plenty of surviving examples, such as Roodstown and Milltown in Co Louth and Dunsoghly, Athgoe and Dalkey in Co Dublin. By 1449 Parliament decided enough fortresses had been built and a limit was placed on new constructions.

Among the largest of the Irish tower houses are at Blarney, Co Cork, Ballycarbury, Co Kilkenny, and Donegal and Greencastle, both Co Donegal. All of these are late 15th century and Donegal became a model for many later towers in Connacht and Munster. Its design placed the great hall on the top storey, allowing it to have narrower walls and bigger windows — features which would have compromised the tower's defensive integrity further down. This arrangement allowed the hall to have a central hearth with a smoke hole in the roof. Munster also has some very fine round tower castles, such as Ballynahow and Newtown.

From the 1580s onwards some new towers were built by settlers on the plantations of Munster and Ulster. However Elizabethan and Jacobean manor houses with no fortifications — a common sight in England and Wales — were unpopular. English families wanting more room and comfort than a tower, but still concerned about defence, would compromise by building stronghouses. These were strengthened by additional wings to permit all-round fire, open wall walkways, turrets, machicolations and pistol-firing positions beneath main windows. Good examples include Rathfarnham, Co Dublin,

Above: *The remains of Carrigogunnell Castle, Co Limerick, which stand on a volcanic crag overlooking the River Shannon. It has a fascinating history and saw action in both the Cromwellian Wars and during the Glorious Revolution.*

Opposite: *Odeas Castle, near Corofin, Co Clare.*

Portumna, Co Galway, Raphoe, Co Donegal, Kanturk, Co Cork, Burncourt, Co Tipperary, and Manorhamilton, Co Leitrim.

Although castles are traditionally seen as family seats, their ownership changed hands many times through force of arms. Ballymote, Co Sligo, is a case in point. It was built around 1300 for Richard de Burgo, fell to the O'Connors soon afterwards and then to the MacDiarmadas. It was later re-claimed by O'Connor and surrendered to the English in 1571. In between times it was held by the MacDonaghs, who lost it to Richard Bigham in 1584. In 1588 it was burnt by the O'Connors, then recaptured by the MacDonaghs in 1598, sold to the O'Donnells and, in 1602, handed over to the English. The Taaffe family then held it from 1630-1652, it was retaken for a time by Captain Terence MacDonagh and re-captured at the end of the 17th century by Lord Granard. After all that, one can only admire as foolhardy any attempt to establish the identity of the 'real' owners.

Above: *Cahir Castle, Co Tipperary. The castle dates from the 13th century but its most impressive fortifications were added during the 15th and 16th centuries. In its heyday it was regarded as one of the strongest castles in Ireland and rebellious owners caused grave problems for Queen Elizabeth I's government.*

Left: *Leamaneh Castle, Co Clare. Legend has it that the widowed lady of the house kicked a Cromwellian soldier out of an upper window.*

Opposite: *Fitzmaurice Castle, Ballybunion, stands in lonely vigil above the Co Kerry coastline.*

*Bunratty Castle, Co Clare, was founded in 1277 by the
Norman lord Sir Thomas de Clare. It withstood four Irish
attacks but by 1306 had been burnt twice.*

Above: *The remains of Ballintubber Castle, Co Roscommon, which became a key centre for Catholic resistance during the war against Cromwell. In 1642 it held out against the government forces of both Lord Raneleagh and Sir Charles Coote.*

Left: *The magnificent interior of Bunratty Castle.*

Opposite: *Until 1922, 13th-century Dublin Castle was the centre for English government in Ireland.*

Above: *A view across the old walled garden at Leamaneh Castle.*

Left *The huge tower of Blarney Castle, Co Cork, which is said to conceal a secret underground passage.*

Opposite: *The elegant castle and gardens at Ayesha, Dalkey, Co Dublin.*

Above: *Ormond Castle at Carrick on Suir, Co. Tipperary*

Left: *Perhaps Ireland's best known piece of folklore involves the kissing of the Blarney stone. The stone forms one of the massive lintels supporting the castle's parapet and the kisser has to dangle upside down through a gap in the walls. For those who accomplish the feat, the reward is said to be 'the gift of the gab'.*

Opposite: *A general view of Blarney Castle.*

Athlone Castle, Co Westmeath.

Opposite: *Whytes Castle at Athy, Co Kildare.*

Above: *The ruins of Carrigogunnell. It was surrendered to Lord Deputy Grey in 1536 by Mahon O'Brien and eventually passed to Michael Boyle, later Archbishop of Dublin. The castle was blown up by General Ginckell in 1691.*

Right: *One of Ireland's most beautiful hillforts — the Grianan of Aileach, Co Donegal.*

Overleaf: *Another view of Ballintubber Castle, Co Roscommon.*

THE GAELIC REVIVAL – IRELAND IN THE 14TH AND 15TH CENTURIES

By the early 14th century the haphazard powerbase of the Norman (now known as English) barons was already breaking down. No longer were they first call when the king's Irish administrators needed military muscle. As often as not, this work would be contracted out to whoever's personal army was (a) capable, and (b) not in a state of revolt. This amounted to the privatisation of the military and it became increasingly difficult to tell the sides apart.

Among the competing forces were, of course, the native Gaelic chieftains. But there were also the 'kerns', small mercenary bands who fostered their barbarian image by going barefoot into battle, and the galloglass — Scottish mercenaries from the Western Isles. The only certain thing was that the English no longer held overall battlefield superiority.

For the ordinary Irishman, this chaotic organisation served only to make the wearying process of earning a living still harder. The Crown began to franchise out tax collection to any two-bit landowner with a small private army. Such a system of 'coign and livery' effectively gave the agents free rein to collect their own income and, unsurprisingly, it became a glorified protection racket. From 1297 onwards the Crown recognised this by limiting the spread of armies to the wild frontier lands where Norman rule was most questionable. There soon followed a tacit acknowledgement of Ireland's divided state from the Anglo-Irish Parliament in Dublin. Between 1310 and 1366 it struck deals with a number of Gaelic chieftains giving them the right to arrest lawbreakers. These villains could be tried by the king's courts in the 'land of peace' (principally the east), but by the chiefs themselves in the 'land of war' (the rest of the country).

By the end of Edward II's reign in 1327 the breakdown in Irish government had translated into a full blown crisis. Europe's population expansion (and the hike in food prices to which it was linked) had ended and many of the fortune-seeking barons who had so eagerly colonised Ireland were now back home in their more comfortable English estates. As a result, half of all colonized Irish territory was owned by absentee landlords. This in turn led to bitterness among those English lords who stayed. They accused their compatriots of failing to maintain armies and defences; thus allowing the native Irish to regain the initiative.

The rise of Scottish nationalism added a further complication. In 1314 Robert the Bruce, king of the Scots, won his great victory at the Battle of Bannockburn, routing the English forces. Robert was keen to consolidate and extend his power and had long been sounding out both the native Irish and the English colonists for support. But when in May 1315 he despatched an army headed by his brother Edward to invade Ulster, he made a basic political blunder.

The Scots claimed to be supporting the revolt of the Irish king Donal O'Neill. This immediately alienated the English colonists, despite the fact that Robert the Bruce was related through marriage to one of their most senior figures — the Red Earl of Ulster. Instead of uniting both the native Irish and discontented English colonists against London, the Scottish army turned them against each other. Edward Bruce was defeated by the English baron John de Bermingham at the Battle of Faughart, Co Louth, in 1318. By then much of the country had been devastated, a situation made worse by a succession of bad winters and a famine in northern Europe.

For Robert the Bruce, defeat in Ireland was little more than a setback. In 1328 the English throne formally recognised Scotland as an independent state and a more peaceful period lay ahead. But in Ireland the chaos continued. Throughout the rest of the century a constant stream of complaints were sent winging across the Irish Sea to London. The Anglo-Irish Parliament warned of crumbling defences and of don't-care absentee landlords; of incompetent crown administrators and of the complete disintegration of the colony's economy. The result, warned Parliament, would be an unstoppable rise of the Gaelic chieftains and the increasing defection of the so-called 'degenerates' — English noblemen rallying to the Irish cause.

These forecasts proved disturbingly close to the mark. The spread of the Black Death in 1348-9, coming so soon after failed harvests and a general collapse in agricultural fortunes, resulted in colonists of all backgrounds heading back to England in the hope of reviving their fortunes. Irish taxes could no longer be relied upon by the English exchequor as easy income.

There were a number of attempts to stop the rot. Edward III and later Richard II, mounted a series of military expeditions aimed at whipping the Irish kings and the English rebels into line. But it was a hopeless task as well as a huge drain on resources. One of the worst ideas was to surround rebel territory with strategically-placed garrisons able to react instantly to any sign of trouble. These castles succeeded in quieting rebel voices. But they proved fantastically expensive to maintain and failed to re-conquer so much as a metre of land for the forces of 'civilisation' and the king. Already at court, talk of the 'Irish Problem' was commonplace.

Opposite: *A weathered portrait stares from the walls of Drumlane Church, Co Cavan.*

The Irish, naturally, were jubilant. Here at last was the long-promised renaissance of the Celts, a chance to re-assert national identity and unite with the rebel English to drive the crown out. A poem written for the inauguration of King Niall Mór O'Neill in 1364 began:

Ireland is a woman risen again
from the horrors of reproach...
she was owned for a while by foreigners
she belongs to Irishmen after that

Well, sort of. As with many aspects of Irish nationalism, the 14th century Gaelic resurgence was not anywhere near so clear-cut. Far from concentrating their efforts against the Crown, the Irish chiefs spent a great deal of time squabbling among themselves. This was understandable, given the way they had been governed by the English barons. The barons had adopted a divide and rule policy, giving every Irish leader equal status — irrespective of claims that certain kings were more important that others. With the old system in disarray, the Irish were once again free to contest rights to over-lordship of the regions. Feuds enshrined in centuries of folklore were duly dusted down by a new generation of rulers.

This twist in Ireland's internal politics brought about a revival of Gaelic culture, particularly poetry and history. The 'praise-poets', responsible for fawning odes on the greatness of various leaders, were highly valued as medieval public relations men. Historians, meanwhile, strove to show how certain lands were the legitimate property of a particular patron king. But the downside of Gaelic ascendancy was evident in the devastating internecine warfare which plagued the lives of ordinary folk. Parts of Ulster and Munster, previously fertile agricultural pastureland, became virtually deserted in the turmoil.

The result of all this was that native the Irish as well as the English rebels wasted men and vast resources in pursuit of often impossible goals, while the Crown virtually abandoned hope of squeezing additional wealth out of the colony. The only real winners were the Anglo-Irish nobility, namely the loyal Crown subjects and government administrators who ran things in the east. Although they had lost territory, they retained a secure stronghold in the counties of Louth, Meath, Dublin and Kildare. To emphasise the point they built the Pale, a defensive earthen rampart designed to keep out the barbarians lurking in the rest of the country. This monument later provided the English language with one of its most useful clichés; the phrase 'beyond the Pale' signifies anything that goes outside the bounds of civilised behaviour.

Gradually, as the warring factions of the native Irish settled down, the dawn of the 15th century brought the beginning of a new stability — even prosperity. There was a trend to build fortified houses and stone towers in every kingdom, (in a total contrast to the neglect of defences in the 14th century) and this suggests that definable kingdoms had become established. Trade with Europe strengthened and many new churches were built by the Gaelic chieftains.

The old English barons, quietly comfortable within the Pale, were by now busily re-inventing their 'Irishness'. They heaped money on their own poets and historians who obligingly assured them that they had as much a stake in national identity as did any Irish king. Surely, it was argued, the early English colonists were no different to the Gaelic traveller of a few centuries earlier. Both were

invaders turned settlers. Both engaged in intermarriage and sought private land rights. Therefore it followed that the two peoples had a common heritage. It was simply that the men of the Pale had ended up wealthier! Convenient as this reasoning may have been it was, as we have seen, historically flawed. There was no Gaelic 'invasion' as such. But there was certainly a Norman conquest, however arbitrary.

As the century drew on there became a growing realisation in England that the mere passing of new laws was never going to bring Irish rebels to heel. Apart from anything else there were more important things to consider — continental campaigns and internal English treason to name but two. The Crown adopted a policy of benign neglect. It wanted to rule Ireland but it wasn't going to get embroiled in a vastly expensive military conflict which promised neither economic nor political rewards. It was content to leave things to the Lords of the Pale, the barons whose family roots were in England and whose ancestors were the first Norman colonists. They could always be counted upon to give unquestioned loyalty to the English king.

This of course was true. But the Old English — as historians confusingly call the barons — had their own agenda. They knew they were held in contempt by the native Irish and that old grudges dating back to the days of the Norman invasion were still nurtured. They expected Irish attacks on their outposts and they were by no means disappointed. However, rather than throw themselves at the mercy of a disinterested king across the Irish Sea, they made alliances amongst themselves, turning those more powerful lords into unofficial protectors of the Old English community. It was to these leaders that allegiance was owed, not the Crown, and they fostered intense loyalty among their followers. They maintained well-trained armies, built strong castles and towers and mounted attacks on any Irish chieftain who came too close.

By the early 16th century, the FitzGerald earls of Kildare had emerged above the Butler earls of Ormond as the most dominant Old English force. The advantages of harnessing the FitzGeralds' political and military power was not lost on Henry VII and Henry VIII, who successively appointed them crown agents responsible for raising the king's taxes and ensuring good government. While this seemed to re-assert the authority of the English kings, in fact the reverse was true. The Kildares made clear that should they not be confirmed as Lord Lieutenants, even the 'loyal' Old English areas of Ireland would become ungovernable. On the odd occasions they were sacked, they proved this to be no empty threat.

Opposite: *The city of Kilkenny saw the passing of the 1366 statutes which reinforced English colonial law on an area regarded as an outpost of civilisation.*

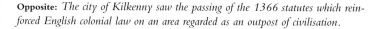

IRELAND IN THE REFORMATION

King Henry VIII's refusal to accept the authority of the Pope put further strain on relations between the Crown and its more loyal Irish subjects. These Old English Catholic families wanted nothing to do with Henry's Reformation, and campaigned actively against his new state church. Many even removed their sons from Oxford and Cambridge colleges for fear that they would become indoctrinated with the heretic Protestant doctrine. The young men were instead sent to continental universities where counter-reformation Catholicism had already taken root.

For months the Old English agonised over a divided loyalty between their god and their king. Eventually, a group of lawyers devised a compromise in which it was suggested that offering political loyalty to the Crown did not necessarily mean an acceptance of it's spiritual supremacy. It was a good try — but it was doomed to failure. No Protestant king or queen would agree a deal completely at odds with most other European monarchies. Rulers, not Rome, were to decide the peoples' religion.

The result of all this was that whenever a plum job in the Dublin civil service was up for grabs, the Crown would seek a 'reliable' English-born Protestant to fill it rather than an Old English Catholic. This caused great resentment among Dublin's lawyers, who realised that, despite their genuine loyalty, their ambitions in government were dead in the water. To their credit, they didn't go down without a fight.

When the new breed of Protestant administrators began to introduce aggressive anti-Catholic legislation (such as the confiscation of land and property) it was the Old English who travelled to London to plead for Crown intervention. They argued that the administrators were trying to inflame a revolt in which they themselves would directly benefit. Perhaps surprisingly, these appeals were very often heeded by English rulers (apart from Oliver Cromwell). Many an ambitious Irish governor would suddenly find his master plan for solving the Irish Problem abruptly cancelled.

Yet it would be wrong to imagine that the conflict between Protestant English monarchs and the Catholic Old English was conducted in the manner of a polite, theological debating society. There was some out and out resistance and some brutal responses.

The first Irish challenge to a Protestant monarch came in 1534 with a show of military force by Lord Thomas Offaly, son of the 9th earl of Kildare and a leading light in the mighty FitzGerald dynasty. In fact Offaly's motives were political rather than religious — he just wanted King Henry VIII to understand that FitzGerald loyalty to the Crown was conditional on London keeping its nose out of Irish government. There was much support among the Old English for this grandstanding. They saw it as a symbolic show of strength rather than a rebellion. But they soon switched sides when

they realised their king was outraged. Henry called Offaly's bluff by sending an army of 2,300 men under Sir William Skeffington to crush him. The king successfully portrayed Offaly as an enemy of the Crown and of its Old English supporters and exacted a terrible revenge by confiscating FitzGerald lands and sentencing all male members of the family, apart from one small child, to death. This uprising, incidentally, saw the only known siege of Dublin Castle during an unsuccessful attempt to wrest it from Crown control.

Henry followed his success by convening an Irish Parliament in 1536 and forcing its members (many of whom had participated in Offaly's revolt) to declare him supreme head of the Irish church. The country was now in exactly the same position as England and indeed a whole weight of new religious laws, already passed by the English Reformation Parliament, was imposed on Ireland.

King Henry knew that he would have to back his new regime with military force and the modest 300-strong garrison in Dublin was, by the middle of the century, reinforced by a further 2,200 men. It was felt in London that the extra cost of maintaining this army could easily be offset by rents wrung from the confiscated monasteries. But the Crown reckoned without the crooked administrators of the Pale, who squirrelled much of the profit away. When Elizabeth I succeeded to the English throne in 1558 a new approach to Irish government was soon well under way.

The first serious attempts to find a non-military solution to the Crown's problems in Ireland were made by successive governors — Thomas, earl of Sussex, and Sir Henry Sidney. These men were ambitious rivals, each seeking a heightened reputation at Elizabeth's court, and each opting for a very different approach. Sussex wanted to negotiate with the native Irish chieftains, restoring previously agreed titles and land rights but subjecting any rebels to instant and decisive military force.

Sidney was far more aggressive, though he presented himself as a peace-maker. His aim was to dispossess any Gaelic leader who fought against the Crown or occupied its lands. These estates would then be handed to English Protestant nobles, on the understanding that English families would be settled on them. Ancient land titles, forgotten since Norman times, were searched out and used as further incentives for the Protestant plantations.

Opposite above: *Among many interesting exhibits at Dublin's Christ Church Cathedral are the mummified remains of a cat and mouse, recovered from the Cathedral crypt.*

Opposite below: *A view of the crypt itself.*

Back in England, fortune-seeking adventurers began rubbing their hands with glee. In fact this first attempt at plantation was a failure. The English incomers, with their headstrong private armies, caused widespread bitterness among the native Irish and soon a rebellion was in full swing. Sidney responded by drawing up plans to extend the plantations far beyond the lands he'd first proposed. But he judged Queen Elizabeth's response badly. Stung to discover that one of her close friends, Thomas, Earl of Ormond, had three brothers involved in the rebellion, she demanded a full report, ordered mercy for all rebel leaders (except one) and suggested the entire crisis was Sidney's fault. Publicly humiliated, he resumed a more conciliatory policy as governor.

The one rebel who was not pardoned was James Fitz Maurice FitzGerald. He had claimed to be fighting a religious war against his heretic queen and, after a short period in exile on the continent, he returned in 1579 intent on driving her out of Ireland. His modest army managed to attract considerable support in both the Pale and Munster, and won the backing of the Earl of Desmond. The earl's seat — Adare Castle, Co Limerick — was one of the finest garrisons in all Ireland and with him on board, the rebellion assumed altogether more serious proportions. The queen responded by sending a powerful 8,000-strong army under Arthur Lord Grey de Wilton to crush it.

The rebel force's cause was hopeless. Some who had supported it quickly changed sides and begged a royal pardon once they saw the odds against them. Others, undecided about whom to back, suddenly emerged as passionately loyal to the Crown. However, although Elizabeth showed some mercy, she was determined to make an example of the ringleaders. Many of FitzGerald's troops were summarily slaughtered and a witch-hunt followed to root out and execute any Gaelic nobleman who had supported him. In the ensuing weeks the English army went on an orgy of slaughter and destruction in Munster on a scale never seen before in Ireland.

Back east, the Palesmen who had rebelled were hung, drawn and quartered — but not before they had been interrogated by Protestant zealots and urged to renounce the pope. When the bloodshed finally stopped, the government officials running Dublin announced plans for a plantation of 20,000 English people on the lands of the Earl of Desmond. These officials were now hell-bent on passing a raft of anti-Catholic laws, including swingeing fines against any landowner who was not following the 'right' religion.

But if the Crown believed its atrocities would end opposition in Ireland, it was hopelessly wrong. By the 1590s a new threat had emerged. Hugh O'Neill, earl of Tyrone and probably Gaelic Ireland's greatest leader, began expelling government officials from Ulster and quickly provoked a confrontation with the Crown. He raised an army, adopted elements of both English and Irish military techniques, and soon had almost every disgruntled nobleman in the country rallying round. O'Neill presented himself as champion of the Papist cause (a dubious claim since he was not exactly a devout Catholic) and convinced King Philip III of Spain that he could smash English colonial rule.

In 1600, after widespread success in Ulster, O'Neill marched south to harry Crown interests. He journeyed down through Westmeath, burned part of Kilkenny and wreaked further havoc in Cork. In February of that year his authority as 'Prince of Ireland' was acknowledged by the Munster chiefs and his declaration of a holy war won over many commoners. When Queen Elizabeth's new Lord Deputy, Lord Mountjoy, landed in Ireland at the head of a 20,000-strong army he soon realised the competence of his enemy.

O'Neill was a clever tactician and early on he dictated the rules of engagement. As Mountjoy advanced, the Gaelic army taunted him by withdrawing to Ulster across the Bog of Allen — a nightmarish prospect for the pursuing English. Elizabethan soldiers hated the impenetrable woods and unyielding marshes and an absence of accurate maps made their progress agonisingly slow. Where Mountjoy encountered rebel forces, the Irish knack for ambush and retreat into the mountains left his men floundering. And when, later, he tried to force his way into Ulster along the Moyry Pass he was hopelessly outmanouvred by Irish skirmishing skills.

But O'Neill's strength was primarily in Ulster, and in the south his rebellion was much more shaky. By 1601 Mountjoy had brought the chiefs of Wicklow and Monaghan into line and his main ally, President of Munster George Carew, had suppressed much of the resistance in the south-west. O'Neill, backed by military support from the king of Spain and strengthened by the forces of another charismatic rebel — 'Red' Hugh O'Donnell, decided the time was ripe for a showdown with the English. It came with the landing of 4,000 Spanish soldiers at Kinsale, Co Cork, in 1601. O'Neill and O'Donnell marched south to join them and reclaim Ireland for the Irish.

Historians have argued for centuries about what went wrong. Certainly many of the cards were stacked in favour of the Irish allies. They were the offensive force. Spanish reinforcements were on the way and the English army was suffering from sickness and desertion. Yet this battle was to be fought on terms which suited Mountjoy. There were no bogs, no woods and no mountains; and unlike his opponents he had a tried and tested military strategy.

O'Neill's tactics were probably his greatest failing and the cause of his downfall. His cumbersome infantry lines were the result of Spanish advice — and they withered before the onslaught of the English cavalry. But there were also worrying divisions within the allied ranks. As the historian Geoffrey Keating later put it: 'It was the fault of the Irish themselves — wrangling over petty, worthless claims — which destroyed them at one stroke, and not the armed might of the foreigners.'

Certainly, the Spanish didn't help matters with their rather timid and indecisive approach to the battle. Mountjoy's cavalry made their decisive charge in the early hours of Christmas Day 1601. Nine days later the besieged rebel force in Kinsale surrendered and O'Neill was defeated.

Mountjoy attempted to rub salt into Irish wounds by symbolically smashing the ancient Stone of Tullahogue, the stone upon which generations of O'Neill kings had been crowned. And yet O'Neill himself salvaged his dignity. In the years following James I accession to the throne (1603) he was confirmed as Earl of Tyrone with all property and land rights intact. In one of those strange twists of history it was O'Neill's old foe Mountjoy, now a senior Crown adviser on Ireland, who fought so hard to ensure he retained his rightful status.

Opposite: *Ruins of a medieval church at Dromineer. The Earl of Ormond became the lord of the manor in 1556 when he took possession of the castle.*

Overleaf: *Christ Church Cathedral as it appears today.*

OLIVER CROMWELL

However well Hugh O'Neill came out of the 1600 rebellion, there was always going to be a Crown backlash. It came in 1607 when James I gave tacit approval for the confiscation of lands and properties owned by rebel Catholics and for new plantations of English Protestants. As ever, Ireland's government officials wasted no time in implementing anti-Catholic laws; laws which they believed would ultimately bring the whole island under the sway of Protestantism. They arranged plantations as far afield as Wexford, Leitrim, Longford, Clare and Tipperary. More significantly, they singled out six of the nine counties of Ulster for Protestant colonization. The religious intolerance which followed (and despite the apologists who say we should not judge past deeds by modern standards, intolerance is the right word) still reverberates today across the island of Ireland.

The rush to join the plantations was unprecedented. In the three decades leading up to 1641 at least 100,000 English, Scottish and Welsh settlers migrated across the Irish Sea. The incomers were handed confiscated land and promptly showed how good they were at confiscating even more. Any patch of territory with an uncertain land title was claimed for the Crown, and therefore for the settler. This phenomena was particularly common in Munster, but not a single Irish county escaped the clutches of some rapacious British landowner.

A fact sometimes forgotten by Irish nationalists however is that native Irish landowners actively assisted this process to feather their own nests. These noblemen wanted to be seen as loyal subjects of the Crown because they saw how wealthy it would make them. By settling English families on their estates they qualified for handsome cash sums and could be assured that their farms would be well maintained and improved. With the money thus acquired, they worked hard to portray themselves for all the world as English gentlemen — building English style manor houses, riding in ornate carriages, commissioning stonemasons to create family vaults and dressing in the latest London fashions.

From 1633 on, the plantation policy moved into overdrive. The new Irish Governor, Thomas Wentworth, made clear that he was looking to begin a new wave of land confiscations and Catholic landowners were tartly informed that they could not expect the king to back them against the more aggressive Protestant incomers. In 1641, believing they faced annihilation, the leading Catholic lords of Ulster began yet another rebellion.

Perhaps they hoped a show of strength would be enough to make their point and sway Crown opinion against the anti-Catholic government regime. If so, they misread the undercurrent of anger and bitterness among ordinary Catholic people. What began as a military uprising turned into a bloody attempt at revolution in which at least 2,000 Protestant settlers were murdered. Thousands

Above: *The old walls at Youghal, Co. Cork. In the post-Cromwellian era the town became an important port for the export of farming produce.*

Opposite: *St Canices Cathedral, Kilkenny City.*

more were stripped of their every possession (even their clothes) and terrible atrocities were committed. The slaughter was seized upon and greatly embellished by Protestant zealots back in Britain, to the point where the British believed there had been a general massacre of their people in Ireland. The English and the Scots demanded that Charles I should avenge the deaths, but he had other things on his mind. Civil war was approaching and he would need every last royalist in his realm to counter the Parliamentarian army.

The Catholic rebels, led by Hugh O'Neill's nephew Owen Roe O'Neill, knew they had been handed a golden opportunity to destroy Protestant power and drive the Crown out of Ireland. But their goal was not supported by those who stood to lose most, namely the Old English landowners. They refused to help O'Neill engage the Scottish Covenanter army which had landed in Ulster to protect the Protestant plantations. And with the Scots eager for revenge, O'Neill could not risk travelling south to expel Crown interests from Dublin.

As the months passed, the chances of a united Ireland grew ever slimmer. Once it became clear that the Parliamentarians, rather than the Royalists, would emerge victorious from the English civil war, Catholic leaders knew their cause was lost. In January 1649, King Charles I was tried and executed and the Parliamentarians could at last turn their attention to Ireland and revenge for the slaughter of

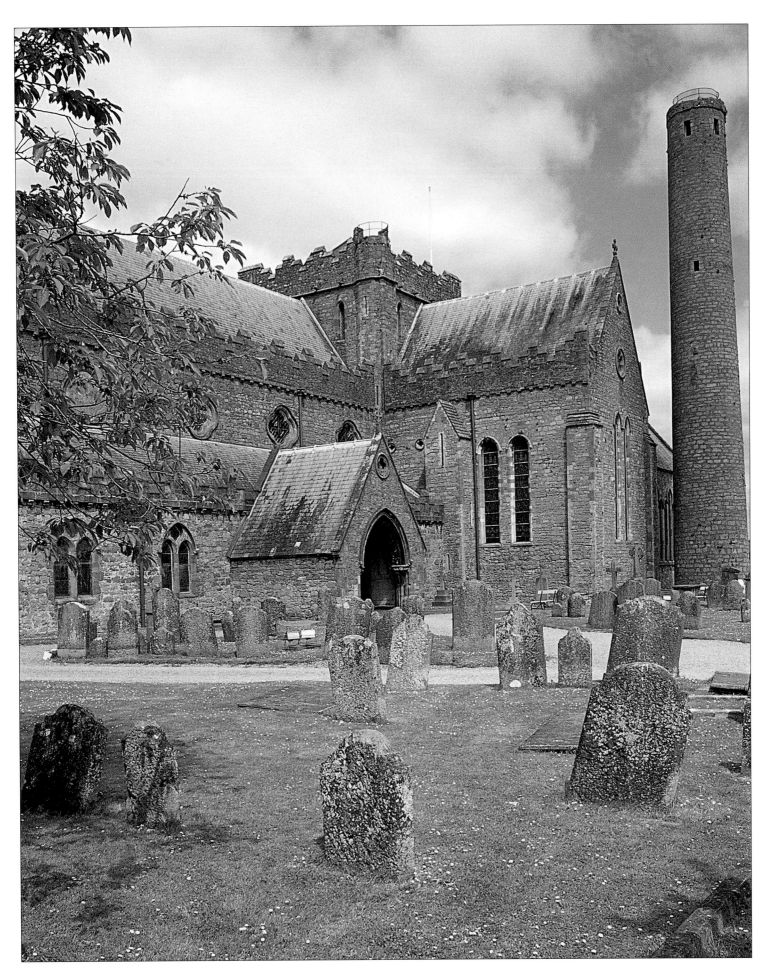

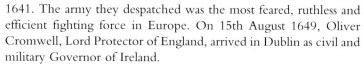

1641. The army they despatched was the most feared, ruthless and efficient fighting force in Europe. On 15th August 1649, Oliver Cromwell, Lord Protector of England, arrived in Dublin as civil and military Governor of Ireland.

Cromwell's strategy was not particularly original. He planned to crush all military resistance to the English Parliament — whether it be from Catholics or Protestant Royalists — and he intended to confiscate the lands of any clergy or estate owners who could be linked to the 1641 rebellion. Further, he prepared an evangelical crusade aimed at bringing the entire country under the Protestant religion. All of these measures had been tried before to some extent in Ireland. The difference was that Cromwell's army was hell-bent on slaughter to achieve his aims.

This wasn't just because his 20,000 soliders were thirsting for revenge and fired with religious motives, although both sentiments played a part. The English infantrymen were also out to fill their pockets after long years on campaign at home. Ireland offered an opportunity to plunder at will.

The atrocities they carried out rank alongside the worst of any army in history. Entire towns were massacred, women and children slaughtered and senior Catholic churchmen publicly executed. Priests were hunted down like animals and the persecution of the Catholic church was so efficient that within a few years its carefully re-organised structure was unrecognisable. Catholic estates were seized and their owners left to fend for themselves alongside all the other refugees.

Some leniency was shown to landowners who could prove they had played no part in the rebellion, although their treatment was hardly just. Cromwell forced them into the poor-quality agricultural belt west of the River Shannon to scrabble among themselves for land. At a stroke, the power and influence enjoyed by wealthy Catholics over their tenants was ended. In their place, Cromwell installed his favoured soldiers and those people from Britain who had helped finance his military campaign.

And what of that campaign? The first point to make is that Cromwell's army was much smaller than that of the Irish coalition forces facing him. Confusingly, the joint-leader of the coalition was actually an Old English Protestant — James Butler, 12th Earl of Ormond. But a common religious belief mattered little to the two commanders. Ormond was an ardent royalist, and therefore Cromwell's enemy.

Ormond had spent the years after 1641 trying to agree a lasting peace with the Irish Catholic Confederates. By 1648 the imminent arrival of Cromwell had created this uneasy alliance and for the exiled Charles II, whom Ormond now represented as Lord Lieutenant of Ireland, there were hopes that the royal standard could be raised again. But the early omens were not good. A fortnight before Cromwell arrived, Ormond and his new allies were trounced by an advance force of Parliamentarians at the Battle of Rathmines in Ulster. It was not until October 1649 that Ormond finally struck a deal with Owen Roe O'Neill ensuring that the coalition forces had numerical superiority.

Right: *Roscommon Castle, Co Roscommon, was captured by Catholic forces in 1645 but was surrendered to the Cromwellian commander Reynalds in 1652.*

Carlow Castle, Co. Carlow. Taken by the Catholics in the 1640s, it was recovered and held by Ireton in 1650.

By then Cromwell's men had already set the barbarous tone of their campaign. On 11 September they stormed the decaying 12th century castle at Drogheda and massacred the townspeople, following this on 11 October with similar horrors in Wexford. Unlike many acts of atrocity in Ireland, which are exaggerated or contested depending on which side of the religious divide you stand, all parties at the time confirmed the unprecedented level of slaughter. Even Cromwell in his later writings seemed uncomfortable with his army's actions, though he never saw the need to make excuses. His supporters simply pointed to similar outrages carried out by Catholics against Protestants in 1641, such as the slaughter of an entire garrison at Augher after it had surrendered (again confirmed by both sides).

There is little doubt that the Wexford and Drogheda bloodbaths inspired terror in other towns, many of which capitulated without a fight. The onset of plague and famine made matters worse and Owen Roe O'Neill's death from an unknown illness in early November was a severe blow to the morale of the Irish allies. When Charles II withdrew his support, the alliance splintered into factions. Its collapse as a serious military force was so rapid that once Cromwell's artillery had battered Kilkenny Castle into submission early in 1650, the Lord Protector began making plans to return home. He finally left in May that year, leaving his trusted commander Henry Ireton in charge of mopping up operations, ably assisted by Edmund Ludlow and Sir Charles Coote.

In the years between 1649 and 1652, Ireland's castles and stronghouses saw more action than at any time in their history. Most of them faced the wrath of Cromwell at some time and to their credit many offered stubborn resistance in the face of hopeless odds. Roscommon Castle in Connacht held out until 1652, but was captured when the Parliamentarian commander Reynalds destroyed much of the northern and southern defences. Athlone, in Co Westmeath, only succumbed after two prolonged attacks by Sir Charles Coote, while Ross Castle, Co Kerry, proved particularly stubborn. This impressive stronghold, which sits on a promontory in Lough Leane, proved intensely frustrating for Ludlow's force of 1,500 infantrymen and 700 horse. It was eventually taken in 1652 after Ludlow's men used floating artillery batteries to bombard it — so fulfilling an ancient prophecy that Ross would remain impregnable until it was attacked by water.

Doe Castle, in Co Donegal, was rather less well prepared, falling victim to Coote's surprise attack in 1650. The castle's owner, Catholic nobleman Colonel Myles MacSweeney, later sent a 1,400 strong detachment to re-capture his family seat. This proved a bad tactical blunder because it weakened his main Catholic army, allowing Coote to rout it in battle.

The years 1650 and 1651 saw garrison after garrison fall to the Cromwellians. Carlow Castle, Co Carlow, and Nenagh Castle, Co Tipperary, both surrendered to Ireton, while Burncourt in Co Tipperary was taken after Cromwell fired the stronghouse and took its owner Sir Richard Everard prisoner (Everard was later hanged). Reynalds and Ireton took Dunamase, Co Laois, the same year. Limerick fell to siege tactics, but Blarney Castle in Cork, claimed to have won a moral victory over the Cromwellians. According to Irish folklore the entire garrison escaped down a tunnel constructed beneath its massive 20m (66ft) tower.

Folk stories abounded in the aftermath of the war. One of the best concerned Leamaneh Castle in Co Clare, owned by Conor O'Brien and his wife Maire Ni Mahon. After O'Brien died in the Battle of Inchicronan in 1651 she apparently saved the family estate from confiscation by marrying a Cromwellian soldier. The marriage did not last long. Legend has it that she pushed him out of an upstairs window after he made some unkind suggestions about her first husband.

At the end of the campaign, Cromwell had good reason to be satisfied. All serious opposition had been crushed. Plans were well underway for a massive new wave of plantations and a framework was in place for the religious 'education' of the Gaelic Irish. This third plank of his political strategy had some success in that Catholics were forced to attend Protestant churches and willing bands of English clergy descended on Ireland as missionairies preaching the 'true faith'. But while this was fine in theory, in many Gaelic-speaking areas worshippers couldn't understand what the new priests were talking about! Ireland's existing Protestant clergy, mindful of Cromwell's excesses, wanted nothing to do with any church run by him. The result was that although Ireland was as Protestant as England in appearance, in reality it remained staunchly Catholic.

Given time, Cromwell might have done something about this; but time was an impossible luxury. The fledgling Parliamentary regime in England was already tottering towards crisis and political stagnation and he needed to devote all his energies to it. The Protestant zealots he'd left behind in Ireland gradually began to drift home, to be replaced by more conciliatory administrators and settlers. Furthermore, many of the Cromwellian military men who had benefited from confiscated Catholic lands soon found themselves homesick. They sold their estates back to the Old English Protestants who had lived in Ireland for generations.

By 1659 Cromwell and his followers were a spent force. Charles II was restored to the throne of England, Scotland and Ireland and many Irishmen — both Protestant and Catholic — believed a new age of peace and prosperity was dawning. Catholic landowners were particularly hopeful of the return of their lands and so when Charles indicated that he would uphold the Cromwellian settlements their despondency was all the harder to bear.

It seemed the only relief offered by the new monarch would be an end to religious persecution and a chance for the Catholic clergy to regroup. Had the Gaelic Irish but known it, their prayers for a true royal saviour would soon be answered. Charles II died (acknowledging his secret adherence to Rome on his deathbed) and on 6th February, 1685 his brother James II — the Catholic duke of York — succeeded the throne.

Opposite: *Another of Ireton's conquests — Nenagh Castle, Co Tipperary — taken by government troops in 1650 following a short siege.*

Above: *The heavily-garrisoned walls of Youghal, Co Cork, a vital trading port in the early 18th century.*

Left: *The courtyard at Dublin Castle. Catholic rebels plotted to take the fortress in 1641 but were betrayed to government forces.*

Opposite above: *The Rock of Dunamace fort, Co Laois was destroyed by Cromwell's troops in 1650.*

Opposite below: *A general view of Roscommon Castle.*

♣

WILLIAM OF ORANGE AND THE GLORIOUS REVOLUTION

James II lived up to his billing in Ireland. He quickly appointed one of his court favourites, Richard Talbot, as Lord Lieutenant and Duke of Tyrconnell with the aim of restoring all Catholic land rights. This was worrying enough for the Protestant population but when they discovered that Tyrconnell was also planning to convene an Irish Catholic Parliament and raise a Catholic army under the command of the king, they began to fear the worst. There was talk of a return to the carnage of 1641.

Tyrconnell's bold (some would say politically naïve) proposals also caused uproar in Britain. His plans were seized upon by a powerful Protestant lobby which was already preparing to 'invite' Prince William of Orange to seize the English throne. The convenience of this 'Glorious Revolution' was that William, a staunch Protestant, was married to James II's daughter Mary, maintaining a tenuous link to the line of succession. With powerful military support, William arrived in England on 5 November, 1688. Eight weeks later James fled — first to France to enlist an army and, in March 1689, on to Kinsale. By now all Ireland outside Ulster was being run by a Catholic administration, and Protestants who had not yet fled north found themselves interviewed and disarmed. In Ulster meanwhile, the Protestant fortresses of Derry and Enniskillen were already plotting hard with William.

The biggest problem facing James and Tyrconnell was to raise a good enough army. They knew they could get the men — Tyrconnell claimed to have 40,000 volunteers — but these troops were largely untrained and inexperienced in warfare. Equipping them was also difficult. Most of Ireland's armourers tended to be unsympathetic Protestants and, in any case, large-scale manufacture of weapons would take time. Hopes that King Louis XIV of France would provide a large, well-trained force were dashed when just 3,000 Frenchmen joined James' Irish adventure in April 1689. But there was no more time for preparations — the siege of Derry had begun.

To all Irish Protestants, the endurance of Derry in the face of overwhelming Catholic military superiority was one of the greatest triumphs in their history. There can be no question of the tenacity and determination of the 30,000 who held out, nor is there any dispute over the hardship they suffered. But the city's achievement in resisting the attackers must be put in perspective.

For a start, the encircling army had never been to war before — let alone worked on siege tactics. It also allowed many of the defenders to leave the city, limiting the psychological effect of this kind of warfare. Protestant accounts tell of the 'treachery' of Derry's commander Colonel Robert Lundy, who fled the city before the siege began, and of the uplifting influence of the fire-and-brimstone preacher George Walker, who took over as joint Governor. Certainly the relief of Derry on 28 July, when food supplies finally arrived, was a massive morale boost for the Protestants and enabled the city to outlast the Catholic troops outside. It was the first major encounter of the war and it won William time to get his act together. The following month his commander, Marshal Schomberg, set off for Ireland with orders to engage and destroy the 'Jacobite' army — the name describing James' coalition of Irish, French, German and Walloon troops.

Schomberg's force, made up of Irish, English, Dutch, German, Jacobite turncoats and (later) Danish troops, was a reasonably well trained outfit, although lacking in military hardware. Schomberg showed little desire to get on with the job and spent much of autumn 1689 riding out cold and wet weather and scouting for intelligence. The Jacobites were equally cautious, using the breathing space to re-structure their army and intensify battle-training. The following spring however both sides were reinforced — French troops for King James; Danish for Schomberg — and when William himself joined the Protestant army a few weeks later all the main players were as ready for war as they could ever be. On 1 July came the moment of truth. The Battle of the Boyne.

The Boyne has been described as the turning point of the war. Yet it was neither a decisive nor a one-sided battle. Although the Williamite forces emerged with most of the honours, allowing them to continue their march south, the Irish cavalry marshalled by their charismatic leader Patrick Sarsfield acquitted themselves quite brilliantly. The battlefield action must have been the most dramatic ever seen by those taking part, with innovations such as cavalrymen hurling grenades and toting carbine rockets.

But it was not so much enemy firepower as indiscipline in the ranks that did for the Jacobites. There was argument over strategy and great jealousy about Sarsfield's reputation (his detractors argued that he was too stupid to be a commander). Whether or not this was true, Sarsfield made up for it by ensuring a comparatively orderly retreat and raising morale when it was most needed. The Irish regrouped at their great western fortress, Limerick Castle, and William's campaign ended on a downbeat note when he failed to dislodge them. On the 5th September he left Ireland, handing over leadership of his army to the Utrecht-born commander Godert de Ginkel.

Opposite: *A simple cross marks the Jacobite camp in the hours before the Battle of the Boyne, Co Meath.*

For the Jacobites the decision of James II to cut and run within three days of the Boyne defeat was a far greater blow. Senior Irish commanders later argued that if the king had not commandeered French ships waiting in the River Shannon to carry him into exile, the long-term outcome of the war would have been very different. Those self-same frigates, it was said, could easily have cut William's supply lines and left him stranded. As it turned out the Irish were left on the defensive, abandoned by their monarch and with little chance of regaining the initiative. When the Duke of Marlborough, a British general, captured Cork and Kinsale for William, prospects for the Catholics looked ever more bleak. These had been the towns best placed to keep open communication links with the French.

By the end of 1690, there were influential voices on both sides arguing for peace. The Old English Catholics, who had done so well under the post-Cromwell re-distribution of land, were prepared to accept almost any terms from William if it meant they could hang on to their property. The hardline Gaelic Irish on the other hand, believed there was still plenty of fighting to be done. Their highly mobile guerilla groups operating behind Protestant lines — the so-called 'rapparees' — seemed capable of dragging Ginkel's forces into a costly war of attrition. Besides, the Limerick-based Catholic army still numbered around 25,000 men.

Ginkel was well aware of the struggle ahead and he favoured a pardon for all Jacobites who surrendered, plus the return of their lands. In his book, the war had effectively ended when James left. A negotiated peace would save money, rapidly get his troops home and avoid the tricky problem of how to take Limerick.

This all made a lot of sense, but to the Protestant hawks in England and Ireland it was quite unthinkable. They wanted their opponents crushed without mercy and so in the early months of 1691 money was poured into Ginkel's army in readiness for the final push. The Jacobites responded by securing further help from France in the shape of reinforcements led by the legendary Marquis de Saint-Ruth. Saint-Ruth had achieved notoriety in Europe through his ruthless persecution of the French Huguenot Protestants (a minority loathed by Louis XIV). His arrival on 9 May brought a new religious passion to the Jacobite cause, although he provoked disunity by his dismissive attitude towards Patrick Sarsfield, his second-in-command.

In June the Williamites managed to win control of Athlone, from where they seemed dangerously capable of sweeping through the entire west. But Saint-Ruth had galvanised his forces and inspired a mood of confidence. There was a plan to outflank Ginkel by re-crossing the Shannon — even sweeping down to Dublin — but this was forestalled by the last great engagement of the war at Aughrim on 12 July.

Aughrim was an unprecedented disaster for the Irish cause. The cavalry, so well-marshalled at the Boyne, broke formation and fled; Saint-Ruth himself was killed, and both Catholic and Protestant losses were immense. Galway Castle surrendered soon afterwards and the Jacobites, with Sarsfield in command, retreated in disarray to Limerick. Their cause was now totally dependant on further reinforcements from the French, and some of the more hardline Gaelic leaders were prepared to hold the city until this help arrived. This counsel was not as reckless as it seemed. For one thing, winter was drawing on and any protracted siege of Limerick would be as uncomfortable for Ginkel's army as it would the defenders. For another, Sarsfield still had many thousands of men and the supplies

Above: *The port of Waterford, on the River Suir. In the early months of Cromwell's onslaught it was among the very few major towns to hold out and was a stronghold of Catholic forces during the Glorious Revolution.*

Opposite: *Mummified remains discovered at Dublin's St Michan's Church.*

to maintain them. With rapparee assistance, he was in the best possible position to resist a lengthy siege.

But such defiance counted for little alongside troop morale. The Irish were battle-weary and increasingly affected by disputes within their leadership. Sarsfield knew that he could hold Limerick, but saw little point, and it was therefore he who approached Ginkel to talk peace. He was clearly not as stupid as his critics claimed, because the deal he wrung from the Williamite General was almost absurdly generous.

Ginkel agreed that Sarsfield's army could be shipped intact over to France, an act tantamount to re-equipping the forces of the enemy. For those Jacobites who stayed behind, however, the constitutional future was as confused as ever. The Treaty of Limerick, signed on 3 October 1691, was so loosely drafted that its terms could be interpreted in any number of different ways. Protestants worried that it was too lenient; Catholics feared it gave no general safeguards for either their property or their religion (although in practice a good proportion of Catholic lands were returned).

In a sense the Treaty was an irrelevance. Protestants felt they had stared into the abyss with events at the Boyne, Aughrim and Limerick and they desperately wanted an end to insecurity. As the 18th century dawned, their power in Ireland would be achieved by a new-wave of sinister laws such as restricting Catholic education, banning priests, denying Catholics the right to bear arms and even preventing them from owning horses worth more than £5.

The single thread that drew this pernicious legislation together was an intent to give Protestants control of the professions, the best government jobs, the best lands and the most political influence. It was the birth of what is now called the Protestant 'Ascendancy'. Today, 200 years on, it remains a key factor in a cruelly-divided nation.

Above: *A quiet stretch of water on the Boyne battlefield site.*

Right: *The grounds of Townley Hall, Co Meath. During and after the battle, the normally tranquil fields in this area would have echoed to the harrowing cries of the dying and wounded.*

Overleaf: *New Ross, on the Barrow River, Co Wexford, was the scene of Confederate Catholic commander Thomas Preston's defeat by Ormond in 1643.*

♣

♣

Ireland's rich religious heritage has produced some of the most beautiful small churches to be seen anywhere in the world.

Above: *St Dolough's, Kinsealy, Co Dublin.*

Right: *The Church of the Assumption, Ballyporeen, Co Tipperary.*

Above: *The stark outline of Baldongan Church, Co Dublin, is a landmark for walkers.*

Opposite: *The supremely elegant St Mary's Cathedral at Kilkenny, one of Ireland's oldest towns.*

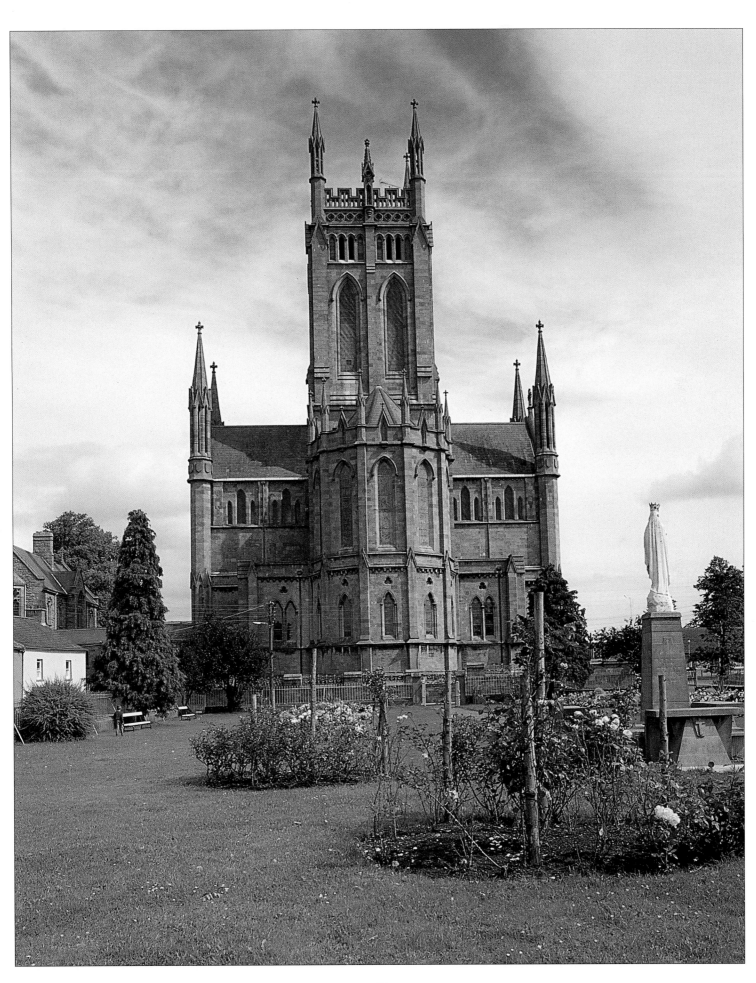

Thatched cottages are an essential and timeless part of the Irish landscape as building techniques have changed little over the centuries. A properly thatched roof is totally waterproof, provides vital insulation and can last half a century.

Above: *A cottage near Lough Corrib, Co Galway. This wild part of Ireland is said to be the spiritual home of the writer James Joyce.*

Left: *An Irish paradise; a farmstead on the coast of Co Donegal.*

Opposite: *A cottage nestles alongside the River Erriff, beneath the uplands of Co Mayo.*

Above: *So neat it could be a model; Edmund Rice House at Callan, Co Kilkenny.*

Right: *Thatched cottages at Kilmore Quay in Co Wexford.*

Overleaf: *Small, but perfectly formed; another of the Kilmore Quay dwellings.*

Agriculture is the lifeblood of Ireland but, despite generous help from the European Community, it remains as tough a life as ever. Broadly speaking, the south-east and east midlands have most of the arable land — elsewhere pasture and hay are the order of the day.

Above: *Cattle wander freely across the desolate limestone plateau that forms The Burren, Co Clare.*

Right: *Connemara ponies soak up the sun.*

Overleaf: *Grazing sheep complete a tranquil rural scene on Achill Island, Co Mayo.*

The beauty of Ireland is timeless and unspoilt. While its mountains may not be as large as others in Europe, they are rugged and beautiful to walk. These pictures show scenes from the Wicklow Mountains less than an hour's drive from Dublin – the haunt of warlords and rebels 'beyond the Pale' – and from the Sperrin mountains of Co Tyrone just south of Londonderry in Ulster.

Above: *Glendalough Upper Lake seen from the Wicklow Way, which runs 132km (82 miles) from Marlay Park in Dublin to Clonegal in Co Carlow, traversing the Wicklow mountains.*

Opposite above: *The Sperrin Mountains in Co Tyrone. View to the south from below Dart Pass to Glenelly valley.*

Opposite below: *The upper valley of the River Liffey, looking south towards mount Mullaghcleevaun (849m -2,784ft).*

Overleaf: *View from the Wicklow Way down onto the ancient monastic city at Glendalough, which flourished for 600 years despite being repeatedly attacked and razed by both the Vikings and the English. The round tower at the site is 33m (110ft) and one of the best examples of its kind in all Ireland.*